Bhakti Yoga Pilgrimage

What Patanjali and Buddha Did Not Teach

Mayapur Samadhi

Bhakti Yoga Pilgrimage

What Patanjali and Buddha Did Not Teach

Sankirtan Das

KAVERI

Kaveri Books
4832/24, Ansari Road
New Delhi - 110002 (India)
Tel.: 011-2328 8140, 2324 5799
e-mail: kaveribooks@vsnl.com
e-mail: kaveribooks@gmail.com

Edition 2016

ISBN 13: 978-81-7479-101-6

Edited by Visakha Priya dasi (GRS)
Layout & Typeset in *Balaram* by *Sparsh Communications, Delhi*
Printed at *Salasar Imaging Systems, Delhi.*

PRINTED IN INDIA

DEDICATION

To the Chinese People
Interested in the
Ancient Science of Yoga

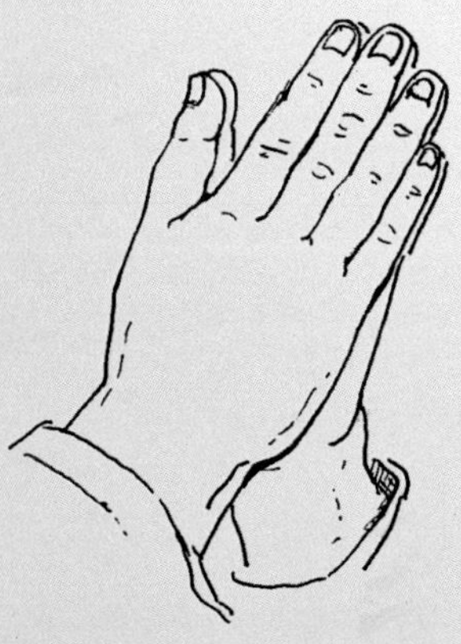

Bodhgaya Risikesh & Haridwar

Contents

Vrindavan

Mayapur

Contents

Vrindavan Town

Krishna Balaram Temple

FOREWORD

The Vedic scriptures compare our world to a vast, fearful ocean of illusion, where the living entities are relentlessly tossed around by the waves of duality. They feverishly grope for pleasure and struggle to avoid pain.

In this ocean of illusion, the living entities vigorously pursue dreams of happiness, just as a man stranded out at sea sees imaginary land and strives hard to reach it. However, happiness remains tantalisingly elusive. Only when the living entity connects to Reality is happiness achievable.

Yoga offers that transcendental connection to the Ultimate Reality, the eternal shore beyond the ocean of illusion. Thus, Yoga is for those who seek to understand Ultimate Reality and the meaning to life; for those who want to make sense of this bewildering world; and for those who want to be truly happy.

But for the lay seeker, negotiating the maze of philosophies, meditative techniques, postures, and breathing methods offered by various schools of Yoga can be a formidable exercise. Rarely do these practices help one to cross over this ocean of illusion, because they are incorrect or incomplete conceptions.

Bhakti Yoga Pilgrimage comes as a breath of fresh air. Sankirtan Das takes us on a stimulating and enlightening yogic journey. He brings a refreshing, yet authentic perspective on Yoga that is complete. It includes and surpasses popular conceptions of Yoga, to transport one to the sublime spiritual realm, unexplored by, and perhaps unknown to, most Yoga teachers today. That is the realm of Bhakti - pure devotion to Sri Krishna, the sweetest, most intimate and complete form of the Ultimate Reality.

Sankirtan Das has succeeded in combining a clear, logical flow of philosophical rigour with brevity in an easy, conversational style. So, dear reader, please begin your journey with all earnest. You will not be the loser!

Bon voyage!

Devamrita Das

President and Senior Counsellor

Krishna-Balarama Mandir, Vrindavan

Chinese Yoga Group

PREFACE

When leading Chinese Yoga practitioners on pilgrimages of holy places in India I often discuss the teachings of Yoga. The experience visitors get in holy places naturally inspires them spiritually. As they observe a different way of life, many questions arise regarding the techniques, philosophy, and culture of Yoga. From the different questions and discussions that ensue, I have concluded that many of my Chinese friends have misunderstandings about the teachings of Yoga.

Of course, misconceptions about spiritual life are not limited to the Chinese. People from many other countries share them, partly due to Indian Swamis and Yogis that influenced America and Europe at the turn of the twentieth century. Adjusting the teachings of Yoga to the different contexts of their Western audiences so they could attract them more readily, these teachers introduced ideas and techniques that deviated from standard spiritual practices, thus compromising the integrity of the theories and methods they were introducing.

To this day the impact of such compromised Yoga practice continues to bedevil us. Moreover, a look at the distorted concepts of Yoga available on the market, will lead one to conclude that commercial interest is a major drive for many Yoga representatives to keep this science unclear. Generally, most Yoga centers give little, if any, education about the profound philosophy of Yoga. And whatever little education they give is usually tinged with misconceptions. Solely interested in the business aspect of Yoga, its promoters sell a service or a product that helps people achieve good health, beauty, freedom from tension, etc.

In one sense, it is very good that Yoga concepts have come to China, since Yoga teachings are beneficial to humanity at large. But only when the concepts of Yoga are correctly understood, will they yield true benefit. Quite often, after realizing how they had not been taught properly even the basics of Yoga, people suggest that someone should produce a book to help the Chinese Yoga practitioners get things right. Such a book should be comprehensive. It should give the reader a broad perspective on the teachings of Yoga, an adequate and well-rounded account of every aspect of the Yoga science, and practical advice that will lead to progress on the spiritual path.

Hence my attempt to fulfill that need and thereby rectify the situation. From my twenty years plus of dedication to the subject I gained an overall objective perspective that allows me to keep the whole picture of the Yoga science in mind and at the same time focus on important details without losing sight of the essential components. I have tried to use my best judgment in selecting what I consider important and of true relevance for a person interested in Yoga and spiritual growth.

The information you will get from these pages is not yet another version of Patanjali's Yoga maxims.[1] Many such books are already on the market, some of them in the Chinese language. The purpose of this book is to help you to develop a more adequate perspective of the whole culture and values of the Yoga science. This book is particularly meant for sincere students of Yoga who wish to improve their understanding of the Yoga science in general and of the ultimate goal of Yoga in particular. It is especially for those who are interested in spiritual growth and who desire to realize Lord Krishna's statement from the *Bhagavad-gita* that after one has practiced Yoga for some time, spiritual knowledge grows within and illuminates everything with its rays. Thus, "one never departs from the Truth, and upon gaining this he thinks there is no greater gain. Being situated in such a position, one is never shaken, even in the midst of greatest difficulty." (Bg 6.23).

This book is meant for those who desire to learn what exactly that "Truth" is and how to gain the position of factual knowledge. You are not advised to accept or reject anything blindly. Everything explained herein should be considered with care and caution. That is the way to achieve freedom from doubt and delusion, and it results in factual spiritual growth.

Fig. 1: His Divine Grace A.C. Bhaktivedanta Swami Prabhupada

Much of the selected materials in this book are from the teachings of His Divine Grace A. C. Bhaktivedanta Swami Prabhupada and students of his such as Suhotra Swami, Bhurijan Das, Ravindra Svarupa Das, and others (see Acknowledgements). With unprecedented clarity and authenticity, Prabhupada (Fig.1) translated many original Sanskrit Yoga texts along with the commentaries of previous great Yoga teachers into English. From studying these works, one comes to acknowledge that Bhakti Yoga[2] is the highest stage of Yoga realization, and that every other aspect of Yoga is to be seen as a stepping-stone to that goal.

Since this understanding is so fundamental and essential, yet at the same time the most ignored and neglected by numerous Yoga teachers, either purposefully or due to ignorance, I decided to make this theme the focus of

1 Patanjali – a prominent ancient scholar and Yoga teacher.

2 Bhakti Yoga: The Yoga of love and devotion – explanations of the different types of Yoga and what they teach is the subject of several Chapters.

my book. Whatever knowledge people have about Yoga usually comes from commented-upon translations of Patanjali's work, but we should know that without giving Bhakti Yoga the actual merit, such commentaries are negligible.

Over the last forty years following Prabhupada's unique literary contribution, many more books and articles in pursuance of his writings and translations have been written to communicate the importance of Bhakti Yoga (see Bibliography). For the task at hand, my work was mainly to choose and compile all the required information and then put it into a structured format, so that the Chinese reader could easily get the benefit of the accumulated knowledge given by Prabhupada and the many other authors in succession. Most of the contributions in this book are duly acknowledged. For example, the chapter describing the eightfold practice of Yoga is entirely taken from Suhotra Maharaja, an accomplished Yoga master under whom I personally studied. Some other minor concepts that I present here and there are not specifically accredited to a particular author but are simply part of a living Bhakti Yoga tradition. Still, if someone feels that I have taken his or her intellectual property, then it is quite accidental and unintentional. I offer my sincere apologies for any type of transgressions.

The book acquaints the reader to places of pilgrimage briefly only, because that is not my intention for writing. The book is a guide for a journey of personal development. For that we dive deeply into the Yoga teachings to find out how they apply to our lives.[3]

We embark with a brief historical account of the Yoga philosophy. The second chapter evaluates basics of Yoga philosophy, thereby providing us with a map for our journey. Although we are like passengers riding on an uncontrollable chariot, we are responsible for the outcome of our journey. Thus, Yoga stresses control of the restless mind, the topic of Chapter Three. In Chapter Four we climb the eight steps of Astanga-Yoga, and in Chapter Five we learn to look at our ascending journey with the help of an analogy, the "Yoga Ladder." Yoga is not a religion but a science and therefore enables one to look at our surrounding with wisdom. Hence, Chapter Six analyses the path of Buddha and the actual significance of his mission. Chapter Seven establishes the direct practice of Bhakti Yoga. As one is supposed to know and follow the laws of any country one visits, we learn about the universal law of Karma in Chapter Eight. How much freedom we have in our decision making is discussed in Chapter Nine; and how one is unable to progress in Yoga if one does not relinquish preconceived ideas (paradigms) - as one absorbed in

3 To learn about holy places in India, I recommend John Howley's: *Holy Place and Temples in India*, BBL, Radhadesh, Belgium: http://www.blservices.com

thoughts of affection for those left behind could not relish a journey - is the topic of Chapter Ten. Chapter Eleven points out misunderstandings that could divert us from the right track.

The goal of Yoga, linking with the Isvara, requires at least a theoretical understanding of what the Isvara is; thus we encounter Him in Chapters Twelve and Thirteen. How our journey started in this world is discussed in Chapter Fourteen. The ultimate destination of our journey is the topic of Chapter Fifteen. As with any other journey, our journey is not free from dangers - the dangers of incorrect teachings - against which Chapters Sixteen and Seventeen give us much needed protection. Enriched from a pilgrimage one has much to share. In Chapter Eighteen we reassess the practice of Yoga by contrasting it to concepts of mundane religions. The book ends with an epilogue showing the practical benefits of Bhakti Yoga.

Simply sightseeing holy places and saying "Wonderful" is not sufficient, because Yoga teachings call for practical actions. Although some of the precepts discussed in the book are likely already a part of the daily life of the Yoga practitioners, nevertheless, in order to remain determined and to progress we need to be clear about the goal of our practice. We need to learn things correctly. Incorrect thinking results in mistaken action, and mistaken actions become habits. Habits become traditions, and in this way entire masses end up living a misdirected way of life.

In former times people learned about Yoga from Yoga teachers and Sanskrit texts written by them. Patanjali was not the only person teaching Yoga. One must be conversant with the different texts to get a correct understanding of Yoga. Such texts might vary in minor details, but essentially they present harmonious conclusions. In this book I used a range of such texts for reference, in order to give a comprehensive perspective to Patanjali's text. You will find the following abbreviations to indicate reference for:

- Bhagavad-gita : "Bg 1.1" , stands for Chapter One / Verse One; [4]
- Srimad Bhagavatam: "SB 1.1.1", stands for Canto One / Chapter One / Verse One;[5]
- Patanjali's Yoga Sutra: "YS 1.1", stands for Section One and Sutra One;
- Caitanya Charitamrita: "CC 1.1", stands for Chapter and Verse;

4 Patanjali's text consists of 196 verses, whereas the Bhagavad-gita has 700 verses.
5 The Srimad Bhagavatam has 18'000 verses.

At the end of this book you will find a bibliography and a glossary with explanations of important Sanskrit terms used throughout the work. There are also appendixes with tables of additional information. Now let us begin the journey - a journey that promises to reward us with wisdom and happiness.

I hope this book will inspire many readers to reassess what they presently do and to progress in their pilgrimage in the company of old and new friends.

INTRODUCTION TO LOCATIONS

This book introduces you to four out of thousands of holy places throughout India, namely Risikesh (with Haridwar), Vrindavan (and surroundings), Bodhgaya, and Mayapur. It is practically not possible to visit all holy places, but these four places relate closely to the philosophical content of this book and are, in one sense, representatives of the many other holy places, an appetizer so to speak. Nevertheless, for one who has developed a taste for Bhakti Yoga, Vrindavan and Mayapur, although not well known to the ordinary tourists, will remain the dearest spots in the entire universe. A person with Bhakti in his heart will find these two places fully rewarding and will want to spend all of his allotted time there without wanting to go anywhere else.

Haridwar & Risikesh

About 230 km. northeast of Delhi, on the way to Risikesh, one passes through Haridwar. Situated at the foot of the Himalayan Mountains, Haridwar literally means "the Gate to Hari" (Vishnu). It is the place where the holy Ganges, coming from the glacier, enters the plains and the place wherefrom holy persons that renounce the world ascend to the caves situated higher up in the mountains.

25 km. further northeast, on the bank of the Ganges, is Risikesh, a very peaceful place famous for Yoga and meditation. Many foreigners interested in Yoga come here for long-term training. The Yoga courses offered are for beginners and advanced practitioners, but unfortunately, much of it is business minded, with little spiritual value. The best climates are from April to June and from September to November. Lately, due to global warming, winters here are less cold and one can also spend the winter without excessive discomfort.

Vrindavan and Surroundings

Vrindavan is a mystical place with many charming spots. It is situated 135 km. south of Delhi, just off the Delhi-Mathura-Agra road that brings visitors to the Taj Mahal. Hardly any of the visitors to the Taj Mahal know about Vrindavan, because Vrindavan is not a tourist spot. But for one interested in spiritual progress and Bhakti Yoga, it is an extremely important place to visit. Vrindavan has around 5000 temples and many bathing places along the Yamuna River. Although Vrindavan is a small town with a population of about 100,000, its surroundings are sacred and worth a visit.

Bodhgaya

Bodhgaya is the place where Gautama Buddha attained enlightenment. It is a sacred pilgrimage place for all the followers of Buddha. Bodhgaya is situated between Kolkata and Varanasi, about 450 km. West of Kolkata, 13 km. next to the city of Gaya. In the area surrounding Bodhgaya are countless monasteries with monks from Japan, Burma, Bhutan, Sri Lanka, Vietnam, and China.

Mayapur

Mayapur is situated on the Ganges, 130 km. north of Kolkata. It is the birthplace of Caitanya Mahaprabhu, who appeared in 1486 A.D. to popularize Bhakti Yoga. The Mayapur area is very lush and its atmosphere is ideal atmosphere for spiritual activities. Daily, thousands of pilgrims, locals and foreigners alike, visit Mayapur. Mayapur is famous for its melodious *kirtans* (singings of mantras). Additionally, Yoga teachers from Europe and India run Yoga Guesthouses with high-class room facilities and intercontinental restaurants. The mood in Mayapur is non-commercial and one easily experiences the spiritual world.

INTRODUCTION TO TEACHINGS

Fig.2: Patanjali Muni

We don't know much about the life of the popular Yoga teacher Patanjali Muni (Fig. 2). Some scholars say he was born about 4000 B. C. and others 400 A.D.

Such a big difference of opinion exists because there are no surviving records about his life. However, Patanjali Muni (also called Patanjali Rishi) gets the credit for having systematically organized techniques of the ancient Yoga science into 196 verses (called Sutras) and this work survived to the present day in the original Sanskrit language.Generally, Yoga teachers refer to Patanjali's Sutras to explain Yoga.

The word *Sutra* literally means "thread" and conveys the meaning of a unifying thread, a line of thoughts; a Sutra thus expresses essential knowledge in a minimum of words. Many such Sutras joined together become the book, then also called Sutra, in this case the Yoga-Sutra. The word *Yoga* derives from the Sanskrit root *yuj*, which means, "to unite" or "link up". Patanjali speaks in these texts about the nature of the mind, the impediments to growth, its attachments, and the method for detachment leading to the attainment of the goal of life, namely Yoga (union) with the Absolute Truth. It is not possible to achieve Yoga unless one deals with the activities of the mind. Patanjali clearly states whilst defining Yoga that the main purpose of Yoga is to rise above the disturbing activities of the mind (*Yogas citta-vrtti-nirodhah*, YS 1.2).

Patanjali grouped the different methodologies and techniques of Yoga known at his time into a single outline. He divided his work of 196 verses (Sutras) into four sections (Kandhas) to deal with four basic topics :

a) samadhi = absorption (51 verses),

b) sadhana = practice (55 verses),

c) siddhis = mystic powers (56 verses),

d) kaivalya = isolation of the self from matter (34 verses).

Since the time that Patanjali compiled the Yoga-Sutra, many translations and commentaries have been written. Due to their compressed nature, Sutras require further explanations. Just as the formula H_2O needs an explanation by the chemist teacher so the student understands that it means *water*, Sutras need experts teachers to reveal the proper understanding to the learner. Unless well trained in the subject, one is sure to misunderstand the meaning of a Sutra. Likewise, persons who write commentaries without reference to other ancient texts on the Yoga science commonly fail to present conclusive information. We have to keep in mind how Patanjali's teachings are part of a cultural setting different from ours. Unless we adjust our own minds to the values and convictions of the persons in former times, we will fail to grasp the implications of Patanjali's teachings and come up with a distorted and partial understanding. For example, Patanjali's writings clearly imply that Patanjali thought of the doctrine of reincarnation as the way to explain our existence in the world. However, he did not see the need to assert or enforce it in the Sutras. That understanding is implicitly assumed throughout his teachings and is critical to understanding the goals of Yoga practice.

To penetrate the teachings of Yoga we need to be open-minded and willing to adjust our present thinking to the way our predecessors looked at the world. Our thoughts need to be in harmony with the Yoga tradition that has - at least in some ways - survived to this day. By visiting holy places, one can observe without difficulty that once the culture and values of Yoga prevailed in people's lives. It is now upon you, my dear reader, to take careful note of the various elements that direct us on our Yoga pilgrimage to a virtually forgotten realm, a realm that exceeds even the Sutras of Patanjali Muni.

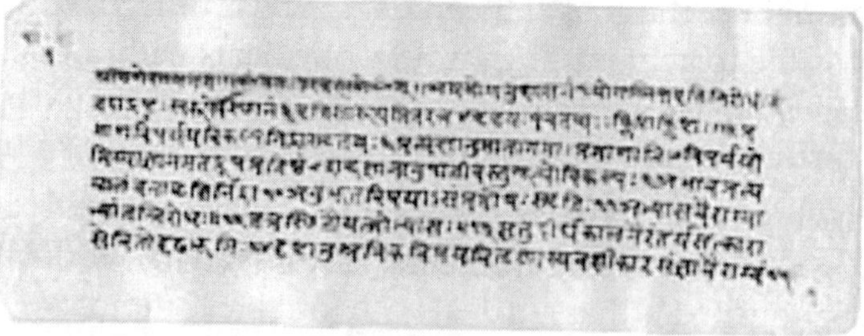

Fig.3: Sample Sutra

CHAPTER ONE

EMBARKING - The Origin of Yoga

The study of ancient books on Yoga leads to the realization that Yoga teachings are based on philosophies far more developed than the philosophical traditions of the West. Even before Buddha, who appeared five hundred years before Christ, India had a spiritually-oriented culture with developed philosophical concepts, and people knew about Yoga teachings derived from the *Vedas*.[6] The *Vedas* teach eternal principles of reality, and such principles form the basis for Yoga teachings. Unlike Buddha, who disregarded *Vedic* scriptures, Patanjali establishes Yoga teachings on fundamental *Vedic* principles.[7]

A. C. Bhaktivedanta Swami Prabhupada writes that the word *Veda* means "books of knowledge." Knowledge is not limited to universities and scientific journals that report on scientific experiments. In fact, real knowledge deals with the subject of eternity.[8]

In a narrower sense - the one most scholars are familiar with - the word *Veda* refers to the four holy books, namely *Rg*, *Yajur*, *Sama*, and *Atharva*, compiled in

6 The word Veda can be traced to the Sanskrit root *vid*, which means, "to know," or "knowledge."

7 Fundamentals are the soul (*atma*), time (*kala*), nature (*prakriti*), action (*karma*), and the controller, the cause of all causes (*Isvarah paramah*). Chapter Six analyses Buddha's teachings and mission from the Yoga perspective.

8 *Beyond Birth and Death: We Are Not These Bodies* (BBT International) Chapter One

Fig. 4: Vyasadeva, compiler of the Vedas

India by a great sage named *Vyasadeva* (Fig. 4) some five thousand years ago. The oral tradition, however, goes back much further in time. The *Vedas* are commonly accepted by their adherents as having originally emanated in an oral form, not from the imperfect human intellect but from higher sources. As the Bhagavad-gita puts it: *"brahma aksara samudbhavam* - the *Vedas* are directly manifest by the infallible." (Bg 3.15). Since the very word *Veda* means knowledge, it is meaningless to debate about the origin of knowledge. Two plus two equals four and we need not research to find out when this fact became a fact.

Based on the eternal fundamental principles mentioned in the *Vedas,* a variety of philosophical systems were established. They are generally known as the "six visions" (*sat-darshan*) and are also counted as part of the *Vedic* teachings because they are supported by the original four *Vedas*. One such teaching is the science of Yoga, which has attracted the attention of contemporary society.

The sixth system, known as *Vedanta* (the ultimate knowledge), was formerly widely accepted as the highest of all six systems, because it deals exclusively with the philosophical portion of the *Vedas*, the *Upanishads*. The *Vedanta* does not concern itself with any feature of the mundane world. Likewise, the Bhagavad-gita teaches one to rise beyond the sections of the four *Vedas* that deal with the temporary world. (Bg 2.45). The majority of *Vedic* thoughts are about living expertly in this world by pious actions (*Karma-khanda*), and as such they are of little value for one who aims at the eternal.[9] A smaller section of the *Vedas*, the *Upanishads*, contains information essential to Yoga and eternity. In a book called

9 For *Karma-khanda* refer to the "Yoga-ladder" in Chapter Five and the Appendix

Vedanta-Sutra, the *Vedanta* system analyzes those philosophical thoughts, which are further discussed in the Bhagavad-gita. These two references are therefore essential for our Yoga pilgrimage.

Fig. 5: A brief overview of Vedic literatures [10] (Source VTE, see Bibliography)

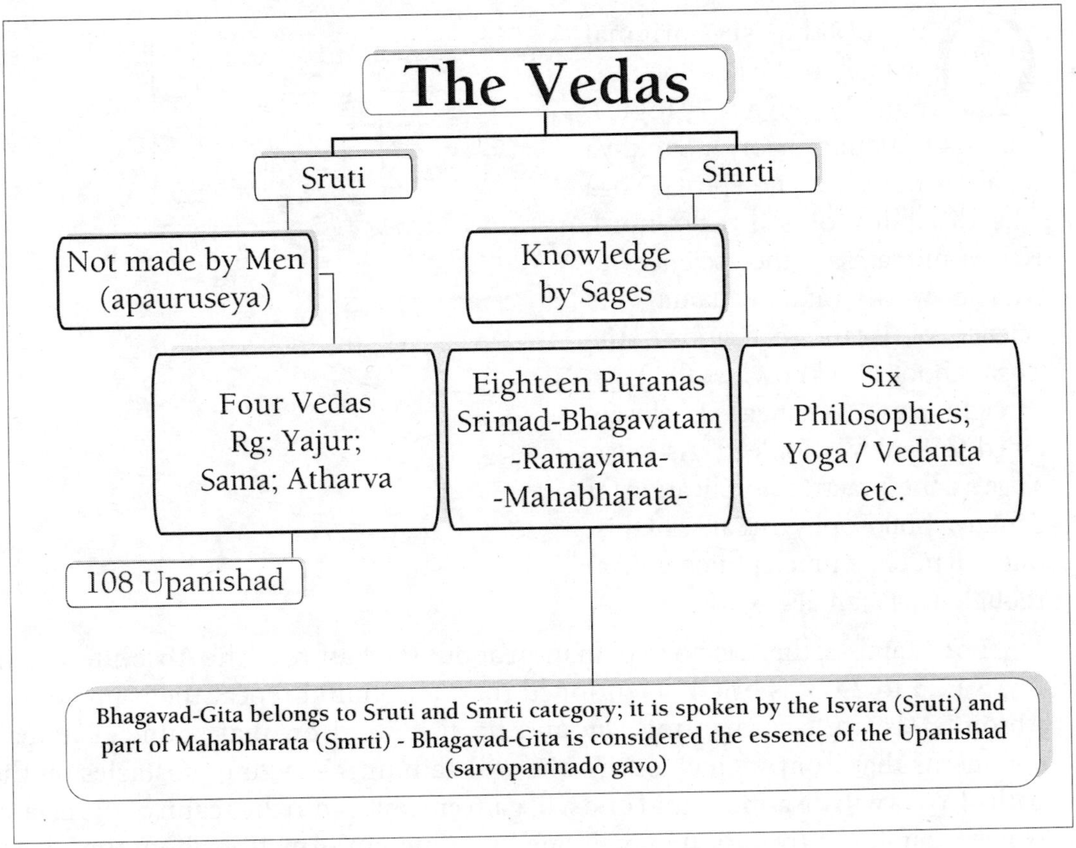

10 Explanation of the terms *Sruti* and *Smrti*: *Sruti* means "to hear" and *smrti* means "to remember." The oldest existing writings of humanity, originating from higher sources, are called Sruti. Based on Sruti, great sages compiled the Smrti, which consist of the Puranas (Srimad Bhagavatam), the Itihasas. (Histories - with Bhagavad Gita as part of the Mahabharata) and the six philosophies, namely 1) Nyaya (logic), 2) Vaiseṣika (atomic theory), 3) Sankhya (analysis of matter and spirit), 4) Yoga (the discipline of self-realization), 5) Karma-mimamsa (the science of fruitive work), and 6) Vedanta (the science of Isvara realization)

CHAPTER TWO

EVALUATING - The Yoga Philosophy

Out of the six original schools of *Vedic* thoughts, namely Nyaya (logic), Vaiseṣika (atomic theory), Sankhya (analysis of matter and spirit), Yoga (the discipline of self-realization), Karma-mimamsa (the science of fruitive work), and Vedanta (the science of Isvara realization), the Yoga school, also known as the Yoga of eight parts (Astanga), is closely allied to Sankhya. Indeed, Astanga-Yoga is the practical application of Sankhya philosophy. Because of this, one will not find much philosophical thoughts in Patanjali's work.

For example, there is no explanation about the nature of the Absolute Truth. In YS 1.24 to 29, it is briefly mentioned that one should repeat the Name of the Absolute (Isvara) by chanting *Om* and fix the mind on that sound. Patanjali comments that from such chanting one will gain introspection, obstacles on the path of Yoga will disappear, and one will gain entrance into the realm of the Isvara. Nowhere in his Sutras, though, will one find much information about the Isvara. Still, Patanjali says that one should repeat these Names and, with one's mind, reflect upon their significance. The difficulty is what to reflect upon when there are no detailed teachings? Evidently, Patanjali assumes that the students are already conversant with teachings that describe the character of that Isvara.

The students in former ages, due to their culture and training in *Vedic* thoughts, had already assimilated the teachings of Sankhya and were conversant with the Isvara by the time they started Yoga practices. Any modern student of Yoga should similarly be conversant with the concept of Isvara. In Chapters Twelve and Thirteen, the concept of Isvara will be discussed in more detail from the perspective of Sankhya philosophy and other *Vedic* literature such as the Bhagavad-gita. The Vedanta-Sutra and the Bhagavad-gita in particular explain that beyond the world of matter is an eternal reality of which the phenomenal world is a shadow reflection: "*janmady asya yatah.*" (Fig. 6)

Fig. 6: The material world is compared to a reflection of the eternal reality, like the reflection of a tree in a body of water.

The Bhagavad-gita further stresses that the Absolute Truth (Isvara), the source of all cosmic variety (living beings, planets, space, time, and so on), must also possess the qualities that are emanating from the source. One such quality, of course, is personality. In other words, the Absolute Truth, or the complete whole (*om purnam*), must possess all the qualities of its parts. For example, the Vedanta-Sutra argues that we are individuals and can feel and think. Therefore, the Absolute Truth must also have these abilities. If this were not the case then wherefrom would these abilities have come? The Vedanta-Sutra argues in favor of a personal (sentient) Absolute Truth. For the practice of Bhakti Yoga, the viewpoint of a sentient Absolute Truth is a fundamental requirement.

It is important to note in this context that many present-day Indian Yoga teachers are consciously or unconsciously deeply rooted in the paradigm[11] of an impersonal (nonsentient) Absolute Truth. Consequently, they comment on the Yoga teachings from a preconceived idea of ultimate oneness that contains no variety and relationship and emphasizes the "void" as the ultimate reality, although there might not be such a concept in the original texts at all. The idea of an impersonal oneness resembles the theory many followers of Buddha hold. It points to a non-sentient existence or in some cases just a simple nothingness (void). One finds this way of thinking in many cultures at different epochs in - and also outside of - India. The most prominent *Vedic* teacher of this type was Sripad *Sankaracarya*[12], who wrote a commentary on the Vedanta-Sutra known as the *Sariraka-bhasya*. His followers still have a strong influence in present-day India and around the world. Such teachers, if they talk about Bhakti at all, present it

11 Paradigm: A set of assumptions, concepts, values, and practices that constitutes a way of viewing reality for the community that shares them, especially in an intellectual discipline. In Chapter Ten we discuss the concept of paradigm in detail.

12 Sankaracarya (or Sankara) appeared in South India at the end of the 7th century A.D. to re-establish the authority of the *Vedic* scriptures and replace Buddhism in India. Refer to Chapter Six.

simply as a convenient practice to attain the goal of oneness; for them loving union is neither an option nor an ultimate reality.

Until recently, commentaries on the Vedanta-Sutra that stress the eternal difference between the living entities and the Absolute[13], and which therefore establish Bhakti, have not received much attention. But with the increasing popularity of Prabhupada's books, which contain such commentaries, the situation is changing. The Bhagavad-gita *As It Is*, currently available worldwide, educates the masses in the personal aspect of the Absolute Truth. The Bhagavad-gita itself teaches the essence of *Vedic* thoughts and contains crossreferences to the Vedanta-Sutra, thereby showing consistency within the *Vedic* conclusions.

It is unfortunate that this original culture of the personal aspect has been diluted and contaminated in various ways over the centuries, to the extent of being loosely identified as "Hinduism." Foreign influence in India has contributed to such violations. Western colonialists attempted to justify their forceful domination of India by labeling her great heritage a superstition, and racism played its part too. Feeling that the Christian culture should replace the *Vedic* culture altogether, the invaders managed to create doubts about the teachings of the *Vedas* in the minds of Indian intellectuals, and they did succeed in educating Indians according to their ideas. Consequently, many Indians have now come to believe that the *Vedas* are essentially mythology. In other words, they think that the *Vedas* lack clarity and conclusiveness and therefore need not be taken seriously; or else, they need to be interpreted in an impersonal way. The idea of an "ultimate nothingness" has somehow made its way into the original *Vedic* conclusions to become part of the Yoga teachings. Thus, it is not a surprise to encounter the same mistaken ideas in the minds of the Chinese Yoga practitioners.[14]

Our Yoga pilgrimage will not go very far unless we rectify this misunderstanding. Philosophy is like a road map - if our map is erroneous, we end up wasting time and energy and fail to reach the destination. Erroneous thinking is the basis for incorrect action. Therefore, one should always carefully evaluate every step in life. Much of the content of this book aims to expose the flaws and dangers of the impersonal view of the Absolute Truth.

---

13 The Srimad Bhagavatam is a commentary to the Vedanta-Sutra. Prabhupada made this momentous literary work available to the whole world by translating it into English.

14 For a summary of the European attitude and impact on India see "*The First Indologists*," a chapter of "*Elements of Vedic Thought and Culture*" (Satsvarupa dasa Goswami) published by BBT international and "*Searching For Vedic India*" (Devamrita Swami) by the same publisher.

CHAPTER THREE

RIDING ON - The Chariot of the Mind

Let us understand what Patanjali's teachings regarding the functioning of the mind are. Patanjali dedicated much of his teachings to explain the nature and character of what we in English call mind.

According to a popular Yoga analogy[15], the mind is compared to a vast lake on the surface of which many different kinds of waves arise. Depending on the size, strength, and speed of the waves, the inner calm state of the lake is obscured to a greater or lesser degree. Similarly, deep within, the mind is always calm and pure, but thoughts stir it into activity. It is not too difficult to calm down the wave-like thoughts on the surface of the lake of the mind, but it is very difficult to calm down those waves of thought that arise from the bottom. Memories are like time bombs buried in the lakebed of the mind. They explode at certain times and disturb the entire lake. When the waves of a lake are still and the water is clear, one can look deep down and see the bottom of the lake. Similarly, when one's thoughts are calm and pure, one can access the innermost potentials hidden deep within.

The mind we have experience of in the phenomenal world is in fact a foreign element; to be under the influence of such a mind is not our normal condition. This mind is a product of impure consciousness through which we experience ourselves in much the same way one perceives an object through its mirrored reflection. In other words we experience ourselves in a perverted way: instead of seeing ourselves as eternal persons (*atma* or soul)[16] we see ourselves as temporary beings. When the lake is calm, the mirror disappears and we are aware of the

---

15 John Harvey, *The Quiet Mind: Transforming Stress* (Himalayan Institute Press, 1988) p.87

16 *Atma* is the Sanskrit word for "individual person". The word "soul" is a misnomer in many instances. In this book, the word "soul" always means *atma*.

Isvara (*Paramatma feature*) that resides next to us (Fig. 7) That Isvara is the source of all our potentials and is our best friend. In later chapters, it will become clear that the *Paramatma* is one aspect of the Absolute Truth.

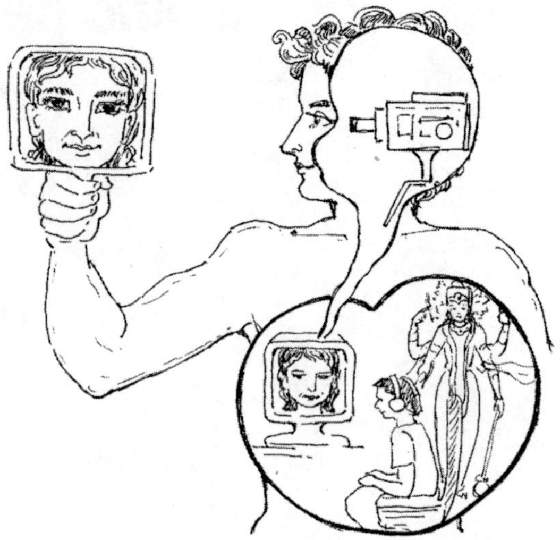

Fig.7: This is the situation of a person in the phenomenal world. He sees himself in the mirror reflection of the mind, and is thus unaware of the Paramatma, his real friend. The person is forgetful of his identity and selfishly absorbed in the external world, the world of matter.

Patanjali uses the Sanskrit word *citta* for what some call "consciousness" and others call "mind." In the analogy, we compared *citta* to the appearance of a vast lake disturbed by waves. The term *mind* does not really cover the meaning of *citta*, a word derived from the root *cit*, meaning "to perceive." *Citta* includes the idea of consciousness whereas *mind* refers mainly to functions of the mind, namely thinking, feeling, and willing. *Citta* stands for both, the lake in the calm condition and the lake agitated by waves.

It is not that the brain-organ (the neurons) produces *citta*. A person in a coma or with no brain-substance can still be conscious, although the functions of the mind may have stopped. *Citta* is a symptom of the *atma* (soul) and disappears from the body only when the *atma* leaves the body - an event commonly known as death.

To adequately translate *citta* into any language is difficult. In Chinese, some use *yishi* and others *zhejeu*. However, both words are somewhat insufficient to cover the full range of implication. Patanjali however has much to say about *citta*, because the *citta* is the basis for bondage (YS 1.5-11) and also the basis for liberation by means of *kaivalyam*, or nonattachment (YS 3.55).

The significance of the right condition of consciousness is also explained in the *Bhagavad-gita*. Instead of *citta* the word there sometimes is *manah* (mind). However, the theory is the same: "The mind is the best friend for one who has conquered him or it is an enemy for one who has failed to do so." (Bg 6.6). Again, in other places in the Bhagavad-gita, the word *citta (or cetah)* is used and Prabhupada chose to translate it as *mind*: *ananya-cetah* - "without deviation of the mind" (Bg 8.14). Whatever the term, *manah* or *citta*, in every case it refers to a state of awareness.

The Bhagavad-gita explains further that the mind, combined with intelligence and false ego, make up the subtle material body (Bg 7.4). Within that subtle body is the real person, the real ego: the spirit soul (*atma*). Consequently, a person who knows himself as soul will direct his awareness (mind) away from things that bind him, and instead focus on becoming one-pointed and pure (Bg 3.43). Yoga philosophy maintains that originally every living being (including animals, plants, insects, aquatics, etc) is a spiritual person with pure *citta* now covered by different layers of subtle and gross energy that repeatedly transform into bodies of matter. Yoga teachings aim at freeing one from these temporary coverings.

Fig. 8: Riding on the chariot made of senses, mind, and intelligence.

The relationship of the body, subtle body (mind and intelligence), and *atma* is very well explained in the *Katha Upanishad* (1.3.3-4), which compares these four items to a chariot driven by horses: The senses (body) are the horses; the mind is the driving instrument (the reins) controlled by the intelligence (seen as the driver), which is directed by the passenger (the *atma*). In the phenomenal world, the *atma* is under a magic charm: he has forgotten his original identity and now identifies with the chariot (Fig. 8) or, as stated before, with his reflection in a mirror. In such a condition, he directs the chariot without proper awareness of who he is and what his real interest is. So much engrossed is he in what he experiences that the body (senses) controls him. Anyone who has carefully observed animals can understand the reality of this description. What the animal perceives dictates its action. Humans should be acting differently, but many do not use their intelligence to guide the mind on how to use the senses, and therefore they behave like animals. According to Yoga philosophy, when one has forgotten one's identity as *atma*, one is considered to be in a deranged condition.

We have explained how the pure state of the *citta* becomes disturbed by thoughts. What is it that causes one's particular thinking? And from where does each *atma* get his particular body? The answer lies in the understanding of the influence and workings of the *gunas* in this phenomenal world. *Guna* means "quality" but it can also mean "rope." When the *atma*, captivated by his mirror reflection, engages in action (*karma*), he gets tightly bound to three basic material qualities: goodness, passion, and ignorance (*sattva, raja,* and *tama*). The Bhagavad-gita gives a detailed description of the influence that these qualities have on our awareness (see Appendix One – Chart on *Gunas*).

Our mind-sets; our convictions; our desires; our character; all that we know and do and feel, are direct consequences of our association with these modes. We associate through what we eat, hear, see, smell, and touch, because all around us we find things in the mode of goodness (morning hours, fresh vegetarian food), passion (hectic city life, rock music) and ignorance (clubs, meat). Nobody in this world can avoid the influence of a particular *guna*. Thus, the lake of pure consciousness gets colored by a mixture of these modes; and the different states of awareness we experience depend on the proportions in which these three qualities interact. This is largely responsible for the sudden arising disturbances of thought patterns in the mind which we all experience.[17]

Patanjali in the Yoga-sutra (YS 1.5) mentions five basic states of mind. They are known as: *ksipta* (disturbed), *mudha* (bewildered), *viksipta* (distracted), *ekagra* (concentrated), and *niroddha* (controlled).

(1)) *Ksipta* is seen as madness, because the mind is unsteady and flitters from one subject to another, always thinking about something, being dominated by the mode of passion (*rajas*). It is the state of the masses of "normal" persons in today's world, when they are not in sound sleep.

(2) *Mudha*: In this state the mind is dominated by ignorance (*tamas*). Sleep, dullness, and laziness are manifestations of the mode of ignorance. Often a so-called wakeful person (*ksipta*) comes under the influence of *tamas* and behaves irrationally. There is no definite boundary between *ksipta* and *mudha*, and the *ksipta* state is continually replaced with the *mudha* state and vice-versa.

The two stages of *ksipta* and *mudha* are hopeless for Yoga and are to be avoided. Western psychiatry deals with patients suffering from depression and mania and has to pay much attention to these states of awareness. The modern way of life greatly fosters ignorance and passion, which results in mental disorders. Yoga teachings focus on the mode of goodness (*sattva*) to break free from these stages.

---

17 A qualified astrologer can calculate a person's life and development by taking into account the influence of the planets on our consciousness. Thus, our exposure to the gunas is simultaneous on the subtle realm, namely the influence of planets, who act as agents to effect the result of our past activities (*prarabdha-karma*). Reference: *Vedanta Psychology, India's Ancient Wisdom of the Mind* (Mayapur, Bhaktivedanta Academy. 2007) p. 119-125

(3) *Viksipta*: The state of being disturbed (*ksipta*) described above and the distracted state (*viksipta*) are quite similar in many respects. However, a difference between them is that from time to time, in the *viksipta* state, there are occasional moments of calm and steadiness even within the general overall picture of inability to concentrate. Goodness *(sattva)* has begun to make its presence felt.

(4) When the mind becomes fixed on some external or internal object and thus becomes as steady as a flame in a windless room; when it has overcome the modes of ignorance and passion and is situated in goodness, it develops the power of single-minded concentration, which is called *ekagrata* (YS 3.11, 12).

(5) In the stage of concentration, *ekagrata*, the mind is still dependent on something external to itself, but in the fully controlled state (*niroddha*), there is no longer dependency. In this controlled state, the awareness is in its pure nature (YS 1.2, 2.51).

Success in Yoga requires a one-pointed and well-controlled mind free from all worldly disturbances. According to Patanjali, attachment to worldly objects is the arch enemy of the individual who wants to understand his inner self. The necessary qualities and conditions for reaching the subtler levels of consciousness include will-power, discrimination, and constant awareness of the ultimate goal. To get control over the mind through the practice of Astanga - Yoga is possible but very difficult. The same goal, namely the freedom from the influence of the *gunas* (and *karma*), is more easily obtained by Bhakti Yoga: "*mam ca yo 'vyabhicarena; bhakti-yogena sevate; sa gunan samatityaitan; brahma-bhuyaya kalpate.*" One attains the platform of Brahman (freedom from worldliness) by Bhakti Yoga (Bg 14.26).

We discuss from Chapter Seven onward why this is so and how to practically perform Bhakti Yoga. For now, we will look more closely into the step by step practice of Astanga-Yoga.

CHAPTER FOUR

CLIMBING - Astanga-Yoga Steps (by Suhotra Maharaja)

Suhotra Maharaja (1950 – 2007) is a disciple of Srila Prabhupada and an accomplished Yoga master under whom I personally studied. As a prolific author, he has produced a wealth of deep wisdom and practical guidance for spiritual growth. Some of his books are *Substance and Shadow*: The Vedic Method of Knowledge (1996), *Transcendental Personalism* - Vedic Answers for the Human Situation (1997) and *Dimensions of Good & Evil* (1999).[18]

I found Suhotra Maharaja's minute analysis of the Astanga-Yoga steps essential for an understanding of how to achieve perfection in Yoga. Once you know these steps, nobody will be able to mislead you with some quick version or easy practices on how to become perfect in Astanga-Yoga. You will know better.

The goal of Yoga is to link (*yuj*) with the Isvara, which can be done through the mechanical process of Astanga-Yoga (eight steps) or with the direct process of Bhakti Yoga. Both practices lead to the same goal, both are equal in standards of regulations, but they are not equal in ease of application.

Of course, one may choose to practice Astanga-Yoga by going to a Yoga class or retreat, skip difficult and unpleasant steps, and still learn to sit in yogic postures, practice exercises in breathing, and take part in sessions of meditation. In this way, the "path" has the advantage of being easy, but sorry to say, it is not very effective to progressive liberation from the influence of the external world (the *gunas*).

18 For a complete list of Suhotra Maharaja's works see, http://www.suhotraprabhu.com/library/library.php

Briefly, the eight steps in Astanga-Yoga are *yama* (restraint of the senses), *niyama* (restraint of the mind), *asana* (sitting in the appropriate posture), *pranayama* (control of the vital force), *pratyahara* (withdrawal from sense objects), *dharana* (mental concentration), *dhyana* (meditation), *samadhi* (trance of perfect realization) (YS 2.29). To follow the Astanga-Yoga system, one must practice all eight stages one after another. Thus only does one attain perfection in Yoga. Such strict discipline is required and it is clearly outlined by Patanjali. Let us now look closely at each step.

(1) Yama – Restraints (YS 2.30)

Patanjali begins by giving moral codes designed to bring about inner peace and harmony between living beings. The first two limbs of Astanga-Yoga – the *yamas* and *niyamas* – consist of ten commitments. The five *yamas* (restraints) are nonviolence (*ahimsa*), truthfulness (*satya*), non-stealing (*asteya*), celibacy (*brahmacarya*), and nonpossessiveness (*aparigraha*).

Ahimsa: The term literally means "non-injury" or "non-violence." Generally, one thinks of non-violence as merely restraining from the physical act of violence, but in Yoga non-violence is to be practiced in thought, speech, and action.

Satya: According to Astanga-Yoga, one should be truthful to oneself and to others in thought, speech, and action. The Yoga student is taught to speak what he thinks and to do what he says. Sometimes one lies without awareness, or just for fun, or for the sake of creating gossip. These simple lies are like seeds that create habits that will one day become one's nature. Thus one cannot trust even oneself.

Asteya: *Asteya*, non-stealing, provides a great opportunity for the practice of nonattachment and non-possessiveness. Actually, non-stealing is a negative explanation of contentment, because when one is self-satisfied one is not tempted to desire others' possessions. In such a state, one considers whatever he has to be sufficient, and he does not allow himself to be enslaved by lust and greed in order to attain desired objects by illegitimate means.

Brahmacarya: The term literally means "to act in *brahman*." One whose life's actions are always executed in the consciousness of "I am not the body" is called a *brahmacari*. The word *brahmacarya* is commonly translated as "sexual abstinence," but celibacy is only a partial explanation of this word. Sexual continence in itself is not the goal; the goal is to control the senses in order to achieve deeper levels of inner awareness. Patanjali takes brahmacarya in a wider sense to mean selectively performing only those activities that are helpful in achieving the highest goal of life. Brahmacarya is possible only when the mind is free from all sensuous desires, especially the sexual urge, which is the most powerful and which can be most destructive if not directed and channeled properly. Unregulated sexual activity dissipates vital energy that is to be utilized for the attainment of higher consciousness. For achieving this goal, the Yoga system advises one to organize all his sensory forces and utilize them in a proper and beneficial way. It teaches control of sensual cravings in order to attain inner peace and happiness greater than all transient bodily pleasures. Uncontrolled senses weaken the mind, and a weakened mind has no capacity to concentrate in one direction or on one object. A person with a mind weakened by lust fails to think properly, speak properly, or act properly. For higher attainment, one therefore has to withdraw one's energies from the petty charms and temptations of sensory objects and convert the flow of the life force towards higher consciousness.

Aparigraha: *Aparigraha*, non-possessiveness, is generally misunderstood to mean denying oneself all material possessions, but the word actually indicates an inward attitude rather than an outward behavior. The feeling of possessiveness is an expression of dissatisfaction, insecurity, attachment, and greed. One who hankers his whole life after more and more worldly objects is never satisfied because that desire can never be quenched. One who is constantly greedy for more forgets that it is impossible to eat more than the stomach can hold, to sleep on more ground than the body covers, or to wear more clothes than the body requires. Whatever one possesses that exceeds the essential requirements becomes a burden, and instead of enjoying it one suffers in watching and taking care of it. A person who desires more than what is required is like a thief who covets what belongs to others. Nonpossessiveness does not mean that one should not plan for the future or that one should give away all one's money; it simply means that one should not be attached to what one has.

(2) Niyamas – Observances (YS 2.32)

The five *niyamas* regulate one's habits and improve our character. They consist of purity (*sauca*), contentment (*santosa*), austerity (*tapas*), self-study (*svadhyaya*), and surrender to the Supreme Being (*isvara pranidhana*). These observances allow a person to be strong physically, mentally, and spiritually.

Sauca: In the context of Yoga science, *sauca* refers to both physical and mental purity. Physical purity protects the body from diseases and mental purity prevents mental energy from being dissipated. Physical purity can be achieved easily, but one has to pay close attention to purity of mind, which depends on spiritual thinking, mindfulness, and discrimination. The Yoga system places great emphasis on developing purity of the mind because concentration and inward exploration are impossible without it, and because psychosomatic diseases and emotional disturbances result from its absence.

Santosa: *Santosa*, contentment, is a mental state in which even a beggar can be happy. It is one's own desires that make one a mental beggar and keep one from being tranquil within. Contentment does not mean that one should be passive or inactive, for practice of contentment must be coordinated with selfless action.

Tapas: The word *tapas* literally means the generation of heat. A yogi who burns with the zeal for austerity is able to generate heat from within his body that keeps him warm and fit even in the icy waters of the Himalayas. Therefore tapas is not to be understood as selftorture. The Bhagavad-gita clearly states that Yoga is not for one who indulges the flesh, nor for one who tortures it. A real yogi enthusiastically takes up a life of healthy asceticism. He may thus gradually unlock mystical powers within himself. By these powers, the yogi is able to easily withstand intense cold or to go for long periods of time without eating, drinking, or even breathing. But until such powers are unlocked, it is useless to try to imitate the accomplishments of tapas. Actually, supernatural powers are not the goal of tapas. The real goal is the development of sincere enthusiasm for a life of austerity. But the ultimate goal is Samadhi in Bhakti.

Svadhyaya: *Svadhyaya* includes studying the scriptures, hearing from saints and sages, and observing the lessons of experience through the eyes of spiritual revelation. Proper svadyaya requires discrimination, which means neither blind acceptance nor critical analysis of the sources of knowledge. One should glean the essence of the transcendental teachings and utilize this essence for practical advancement. Without discrimination, one may become confused by the apparent contradictions among different teachings from various scriptures and authorities. Therefore proper study is a skill that must be learned from one who has mastered the scriptures.

Isvara pranidhana: *Isvara pranidhana*, surrender to the Supreme Being, is the best method for protecting oneself from the dangers of attachment, false identification, and the idea of "I am the doer." Surrender is possible through cultivation of faith and devotion to the Isvara within the heart.

In essence, by following *Yama* and *Niyama* one replaces animalistic urges with saintly virtues and thus breaks the four legs of *adharma* (sinful life) which stands on meat-eating (counteracted by ahimsa); illicit sex (counteracted by brahmacarya); gambling (counteracted by satya); intoxication (counteracted by tapas).

(3) Asana – Posture (YS 2.46)

Asanas, or physical postures, ensure physical health and mental harmony. They are used in conjunction with the *yamas* and *niyamas* and the other limbs of *Astanga*-Yoga, for without the other elements of the system, mere physical exercise cannot provide the desired benefits. Nowadays, because many so-called students of Yoga do not understand the importance of mastering the *yamas* and *niyamas* before attempting the asanas, the yogic postures have largely degenerated into mere physical culture.

The Yoga asanas are not a means of improving physical beauty but important prerequisites for the attainment of the higher goals of this Yoga system. The highest aim of Yoga is to attain Samadhi. The meditative postures enable one to sit comfortably and steadily for a long time with the head, neck, and trunk properly aligned, so that breathing may be regulated, the mind may be withdrawn from the senses and concentrated within, and Samadhi (unbroken trance) may at last be attained.

The postures are broadly divided into two major categories: postures for physical wellbeing and postures for meditation. The commentators on Patanjali's Sutras mention only a few postures that are helpful in meditation, but later Yoga scriptures describe a complete science of postures for physical and mental well-being. There are eighty-four classical postures, but only four of these are suggested for the practice of meditation. These are *sukhasana* (the easy pose), *svastikasana* (the auspicious pose), *padmasana* (the lotus pose), and *siddhasana* (the accomplished pose). In all meditative postures, the emphasis is on keeping the head, neck, and trunk straight. When the spine is aligned in a straight vertical line, it provides steadiness and comfort in the posture and minimizes the consumption of oxygen.

(4) Pranayama – Control of the Vital Force (YS 2.49-53)

The word *prana* is derived from the Sanskrit root *ana* and the prefix *pra*. *Ana* means "to animate or vibrate," and *pra* means "first unit." Thus the word *prana* means "the first unit of energy." Whatever animates or moves is an expression of *prana* – the life force. All the forces in the world, including individual beings, are different manifestations or expressions of this life-force. This vital force animates all the energies involved in the physical and mental processes, and thus it is *prana* that sustains and activates the body and mind.

Prana is the basic principle underlying all biophysical functions. In later years, writings of Yoga explain a highly advanced science of *prana*, which yogis claim establishes the link between body and mind and vitalizes both. Because the breath is the grossest manifestation of this vital function, the science of *prana* is also called the science of breath. Continuous regulation of the breath strengthens the nervous system and harmonizes all mental activities.

The science of breath is related to subtle energy channels called *nadis*. According to yogis, the body is essentially a field of energy, but only a very small part of that energy is utilized, and so the greatest part of it remains dormant. With the help of pranayama (the science of *prana*), however, a person who practices (in China Qigong Masters) unveils that energy field to expand or channel it.

The first four stages of Yoga discussed thus far – that is, yama, niyama, asana, and pranayama – are sometimes collectively known as Hatha-Yoga.

(5) Pratyahara – Withdrawal of the Senses (YS 2.54-55)

The fifth limb of Yoga is pratyahara, the withdrawal or control of the senses. In outward activities the mind contacts external objects through the five senses of sight, hearing, touch, taste, and smell. The interaction of the senses with their objects is like the blowing wind that disturbs the surface of the lake of the mind and causes waves to arise.

Withdrawal of the senses is a technique through which a student acquires the ability to voluntarily draw his attention inward and keep his mind from distractions. Wherever there is contact of the senses with their sense-objects, the mind is necessarily involved. So withdrawal of the senses actually means withdrawal of the mind. *Vyasadeva* therefore says that when the senses are disconnected from their sense-objects, they dwell in or dissolve into the mind. Once the modifications of the mind are controlled, it is not necessary to make any extra effort to control the senses. When the queen bee (mind) flies, all the bees (senses) fly, and when she sits, all the bees sit around her.

(6) Dharana -- Concentration (YS 3.1)

Once the mind and senses have withdrawn from external objects, the mind must then carry a single thought in a desired direction. Concentration, the sixth limb of Yoga, is a process through which one withdraws the mind from all directions and focuses its powers for a further journey inward. To facilitate this process, one selects a suitable object for concentration such as a *Mantra*, a form, or a center in the body, to name a few. In daily life, one unconsciously and involuntarily concentrates in many ways. In extreme happiness or sorrow, for example, the mind becomes concentrated on one single thought. But such concentration is motivated by impure emotions or impulse and is therefore not considered to be yogic concentration. According to Patanjali, concentration is an internal process that is directed by full awareness.

There are four factors that are helpful in bringing the mind to a state of concentration:

a) One cannot focus the mind unless one has great interest in the object on which one wants to concentrate. Hence, developing interest is the first step. Interest further develops into love, resulting in full attention to an object.

b) Practice is the next requisite. Regular repetition of techniques that help the mind to flow spontaneously without a break helps form the habit of concentration. For example, setting a specific practice time, choosing a favorable environment, keeping a proper diet, and regulating sleep make it easier to concentrate.

c) Next, keeping the same straight, steady, and comfortable seated posture and a smooth, deep, and regular diaphragmatic breathing pattern every time one practices, helps one keep the mind and body calm, yet alert.

d) Finally, a calm mind is necessary because an emotionally disturbed mind cannot concentrate. An attitude of detachment from external objects and watchfulness over one's own physical and mental activity is helpful to calm the mind and fosters emotional maturity.

(7) Dhyana – Meditation (YS 3.2)

The seventh step in the practice of Yoga is dhyana (meditation). Meditation is an advanced state of concentration in which one single object of concentration flows without interruption. In this state, the mind becomes fully one-pointed, and by one-pointedness the yogi can approach the Isvara.

(8) Samadhi – Spiritual Absorption (YS 3.3)

Samadhi is a state beyond mundane thinking and feeling in which the individual soul is linked with the Supreme Soul. In Samadhi one casts away all limitations and enjoys eternal happiness. It is not a state of the dissolution of individuality. Yogis know Samadhi as a mystical fulfillment of individuality. There are two stages of Samadhi: *sabija* and *nirbija*. *Sabija* Samadhi means Samadhi "with seeds." In this state, the sense of individual interest separate from the Isvara is retained and the seeds of selfish desire and attachment still remain in

latent form. One can be connected with the Isvara only when the *citta* is pure - the mirror reflection has dissolved. In such a state of awareness the individual *atma* is united with the All Powerful. However, if one is not accustomed to always think of himself as subordinate to the Isvara, he falls into the trap of misconceiving himself as that independent powerful. Because of this impure inclination, he retains the mirror type of awareness discussed in the previous chapters. He thus takes pride in mystic powers that in fact belong to the Isvara. Such pride causes him to remain in the material world of birth and death. In the state of *nirbija*, or seedless Samadhi, however, the individual consciousness is completely united with the Isvara. By surrendering all separate interests and serving only the interests of the Isvara, the yogi becomes the Isvara's pure devotee and, by His mercy, gains entry into the eternal spiritual realm (*Vaikuntha*).

In later chapters, we will further discuss the journey of the Yogi that leaves behind the influence of the phenomenal world forever.

CHAPTER FIVE

ASCENDING - The Yoga Ladder

You may have heard of different traditional Yoga systems.[19] However, rest assured that the disciplinary requirements outlined in the last chapter for the attainment of the goal of yoga are universally applicable to each and every system of Yoga. Patanjali's definition of Yoga means a total overhaul of consciousness, from material awareness to spiritual awareness or from self-centeredness (*kama*) to Isvara-centeredness (*prema*). As explained in the introduction to this book, the word *Yoga* refers to linking with the Absolute Truth.

This implies that any genuine approach to Yoga involves the spiritual pursuit. It also means that the ultimate reality cannot be a void. If the ultimate reality were a void, then our present sense of existence would be entirely an illusion, and our relationship, or union (Yoga), would also be illusory. If the void were the ultimate state, Yoga would be a deception and there would be no link to anything.

On the other hand, if we accept our existence as spiritual beings and relationships as spiritually real, then at least two spiritual persons would eternally exist. In traditional Yoga teachings, there are, in fact, two categories of eternal persons: (1) the souls (*atma*) that live in individual physical bodies and (2) the Absolute Truth with His expansions (Isvara). That is the Bhagavad-gita's teachings on Yoga, and we should know that from time immemorial the Bhagavad-gita has been, and continues to be considered the most important text book on spiritual life.

What does the Bhagavad-gita say about the different Yoga systems? Are they all equally valid? The Bhagavad-gita presents a hierarchy of levels based on the degree of detachment from the external world that the system provides. By progressive practice one will arrive to a state of purity free from desire to reap the

19 Traditional Yoga systems are: Hatha Yoga, Jnana-Yoga, Raja-Yoga, Dhyana-Yoga, Kriya-Yoga, Astanga-Yoga and so on. Some people invent Yoga names for gymnastic exercises, such as Office-Yoga or Fitness-Yoga and so on.

fruit of one's actions and on will perform one's actions as an offering to the Absolute Truth. This level of detached action is called *niskama-karma-yoga*, action without selfish desire. In that state one is free from the reactions that bind one to the world because one learns to work as an *agent* rather than as an *enjoyer* - one learns to work lovingly for and on behalf of the Absolute Truth. This is the essential teaching of the Bhagavad-gita. To reach this state one must engage in practices that bring about a pure state of mind. Step by step, the Bhagavad-gita takes us through the different Yoga levels in a way that resembles the climbing of a ladder. The ultimate message of the Bhagavad-gita, however, is Bhakti Yoga and the practice can be directly adopted by anyone who approaches a spiritual master of the top level, i.e., a person fixed in the practice of Bhakti Yoga.[20]

In China, Lei Feng is cited as an ideal embodiment of selfless service. However, Lei Feng is not a Yogi, because his service attitude is not linked (Yoga) to a spiritual goal. Yet there is detachment in his work, and it might lead to more progress. Aspiring spiritualists often misunderstand that an active life is incompatible with spiritual life. Thus they wrongly conclude that one has to become devoid of desires and actions. The Bhagavad-gita seeks to correct this misconception. Positive spiritual actions are recommended instead of inaction. Instead of acting for selfish goals, one can renounce the world by acting for the Isvara. Thus in the Bhagavad-gita, Krishna, who is also known as *Yogesvara* (*Yoga-Isvara* or "the Master of Yoga"), teaches Arjuna not about renunciation of action, but about renunciation of the *results* of action.

Patanjali likewise states that to attain Samadhi one should act in Yoga (YS 2.1-2): *Isvarapranidhanani Kriya-Yoga,* dedication to the Isvara, which means to act (*karma-kriya*) in Yoga.

The Bhagavad-gita gives practical insights on how to perform Action-Yoga (Karma-Yoga). First, we need to understand what our position in relation to the Isvara is, which leads one to realize that the world we experience does not belong to us but is part of the Absolute Truth. Such understanding and awareness was held by great kings (*Rajas* – hence *Raja-Yoga*) in ancient times. They would rule dutifully, without desire for personal gain, but with a mood of service to the Isvara; then, at the proper time, backed up by their lifelong practice of dutiful action in spiritual consciousness, they would retire to the forest to engage the remaining portion of their lives in devotional meditation. Common persons, however, spend their lives absorbed in selfish pursuits, ignorant of the fact that this world within our experience is a perverted reflection of the spiritual world (see Fig.6 page 25).

20 See Appendix "Yoga Ladder" - the direct approach to the goal of Yoga vs the indirect (step by step)

The concept of ascending a ladder, the "Yoga Ladder," is helpful for understanding the different types of Yoga practices and the different achievements. We will now look at a passage from a study guide on the Bhagavad-gita, which will shed further light on the topic.[21]

*****

Every soul in the phenomenal world attempts (either subtly or grossly) to position himself as the Isvara - as the enjoyer and controller. This mentality is true regardless of the body the soul inhabits. The striving of ignorant animals for pleasure according to their limited capacity is the same as that of spiritually undeveloped humans who, in their attempt to taste sensual pleasure, act in ignorance. The culture of Yoga provides a system whereby the materially-attached person can satisfy his material desires yet gradually become purified. Therefore a high percentage of *Vedic* information centers on *Karma-khanda*, the performance of sacrifices and rituals to reach higher planets and satisfy superior beings, viz. the demigods. One who follows this system gets purified because the system is designed for that purpose, even though the persons who follow it might initially have many temporary desires.

Gradually, by following the *Vedic* system, one comes to accept an eternal, transcendental objective to replace one's temporary, gain-oriented goals. With that acceptance, one abandons the designation of *Karma-khandi* and becomes a *Karma-yogi*. By properly performing his appropriate duties, the *Karma-Yogi* will gradually move from *Sakama- Karma-Yoga* (attached work) to *Niskama-Karma-Yoga* (detached work) because of *jnana* (knowledge). He thus moves upward in the Yoga ladder toward Isvara realization, and finally devotional service to the Isvara. The Bhagavad-gita describes this gradual ascension in Chapters Three through Six. In addition to the step-by-step process, Krishna explains what takes place when, either from the beginning of one's practices or on any rung of the ladder, one attains the association of a *Bhakti-Yogi* and comes to accept oneself as the Isvara's servant.

A person who accepts his position as a servant (devotee) of the Isvara, though still practicing either *Sakama-Karma-Yoga* or *Niskama-Karma-Yoga*, is no longer on the same step-by-step path as other practitioners. Although not fully realized and still attached materially, he is more fortunate because he has acknowledged the ultimate goal and will, by steady and appropriate practice, gradually advance in a way that appears to parallel the advancement of other practitioners, but, in fact, is not. Although it is true that both the devotee seeking to reestablish his

21 The passage is adapted from Bhurijana dasa, *Surrender unto Me: Chapter Three* (see Bibliography).

relationship with the Isvara and the selfless non-devotee seeking liberation will gradually see their material attachments loosen by their performance of appropriate practices of, say *Sakama-Karma-Yoga*, the *Sakama-Karma-Yogi* who is in the mood of service to the Isvara is far superior, because he has already begun to aspire for the highest goal: a loving relationship with the Isvara. The non-devotee, however, might never reach an understanding of the highest goal, and therefore he may never reach the highest rung of the Yoga Ladder.

Moreover, anyone who practices Yoga but does not know that the ultimate goal is to please the Isvara, limits his advancement to his own capabilities, whereas one who sets the Isvara's service as his goal attains His mercy and also that of His countless servants, who act as one's support throughout the spiritual journey.

In other words, the non-devotee faces two difficulties: he may never understand that the highest rung of the Yoga Ladder is to attain the service position, and he is limited by his power to advance because he does not gain the assistance of the Isvara's descending mercy. However, the whole aim of any type of Yoga is to make progress to the stage of pure, selfless love (*prema*). One should seek out the association of devotees.

Prabhupada confirms the concept of the Yoga Ladder in the Bhagavad-gita *As It Is*, 6.47 purport: "The culmination of all kinds of Yoga practices lies in Bhakti Yoga. All other Yogas are but means to come to the point of Bhakti in Bhakti Yoga. Yoga actually means Bhakti Yoga; all other Yogas are progressions toward the destination of Bhakti Yoga. From the beginning of *Karma-Yoga* to the end of Bhakti Yoga is a long way to self-realization. *Karma-Yoga* without fruitive results, is the beginning of this path. When *Karma-Yoga* increases in knowledge and renunciation, the stage is called *Jnana-Yoga*. When *Jnana-Yoga* increases in meditation on the Isvara by different physical processes and the mind is on Him, it is called *Astanga-Yoga*. And when one surpasses Astanga-Yoga and comes to the point of the Supreme Personality of Godhead, it is called Bhakti Yoga, the culmination. Factually, Bhakti Yoga is the ultimate goal, but to analyze Bhakti Yoga minutely one has to understand the other Yogas. The Yogi who is progressive is therefore on the true path of eternal good fortune. One who sticks to a particular point and does not make further progress is called by that particular name: Karma-Yogi, Jnana-Yogi or Dhyana-Yogi, Raja-Yogi, Hatha-Yogi, etc. If one is fortunate enough to come to the point of Bhakti Yoga, it is to be understood that he has surpassed all other Yogas."

Dr. Jean Varenne, a Professor of Sanskrit Studies at the University of Aix-en-Provence (Marseilles), France, expresses his view in the following review of the Bhagavad-gita *As It Is*, by A. C. Bhaktivedanta Swami Prabhupada: "It is an Indian tradition that all important spiritual masters explain for their disciples the fundamental text of Indian culture, the Bhagavad-gita. Bhaktivedanta Swami Prabhupada has followed this tradition; and now we have the French translation of the Bhagavad-gita *As It Is*. As for the teachings of Srila Prabhupada, they are obviously faithful to those of Caitanya, the celebrated apostle of a renaissance in Bhakti, who appeared in the sixteenth century. From this point of view, this magnificently presented book is of inestimable value, for the West knows little of this major current in India culture. For many reasons, until now it has been the Vedanta of Sankara, or the Yoga of Patanjali, which have been the most easily accessible to us. These are, however, far from a complete representation of this multi-faceted, complex culture. The Hindus themselves profess that all these paths converge and ultimately become one. Untiringly, Swami Bhaktivedanta insists on this one path as being Bhakti, and that Bhakti is the surest path of salvation (a conclusion supported everywhere in the Bhagavad-gita itself). One cannot help but enthusiastically recommend that others read such a work, which, from so many points of view, merits applause." [22]

22 Back to Godhead Magazine # 12-06, 1977, "Every Town and Village," *French Professor Praises* Bhagavad-Gita *As It Is*.

CHAPTER SIX

WALKING WITH - The Buddha

As people hold misconceptions about the teachings of Yoga, they also do about the teaching of Buddha.[23] And unfortunately, visiting the holy places of Buddha in India often increases the confusion. Hypothetically, at least in my opinion, one can explore Buddha's teachings and mission from the perspective of Bhakti Yoga, as we do with Patanjali's Yoga teachings. Because the Bhakti Yoga teachings are lucid, historically and philosophically reliable, and the parental source of the Buddha tradition, they give one a sound understanding of Buddha's teachings. To benefit everyone on their respective pilgrimage, I included this chapter, which investigates who Buddha was, what he did, the context within which his mission came into existence, and what people do with it. I assure you that I have no bias against any faction or people. My intention in writing this chapter is to eradicate an undesirable blockage on the path back to one's pure identity.

Of course, at the core of all misconception is a false self-identity (*ahankara* [24]). Any identification with something other than "I am an eternal individual soul, an integral fragment of the Supreme Soul" is a misunderstanding. Nobody is a Hindu, a Buddhist, or a Christian, or whatever, although one might follow that particular school of practice. However, we are not the practice! The real point is to make progress, never mind what I'm in at present.

---

23 I wish to clarify whom we refer to when we speak of Buddha: By studying Buddhist scriptures such as the Prajna-paramita Sutra and others, we learn that there are three categories of Buddha: Manusya-buddha (human-buddha), Bodhisattva-buddha (enlightened) and Adi-buddha (the original Buddha). Amongst the Manusya-buddha, or human Buddha, is the Buddha who is the founder of the religion named after him. That Buddha was born in 563 B.C. in the town of Kapilavastu, Nepal, near Lumbini Gardens. His father was Suddhodana, the King of the Sakya dynasty. His mother was Queen Mayadevi. They named the prince Siddharta, and he later became a disciple of Gautama Muni of the Kapila dynasty, therefore his other name was Gautama. He is worshiped in Bodha Gaya, North India, the place where he attained enlightenment. It is to this Buddha that I refer to throughout this presentation.

24 *Ahankara* is the Sanskrit word for "false ego"; *ahaṅkāra-vimūḍhātmā kartāham iti manyate* - The spirit soul bewildered by the influence of false ego thinks himself the doer of activities that are in actuality carried out by the three modes of material nature (Bg. 3.27).

Let us survey what history and common sense suggest to us. In the previous chapters we established that Yoga is not a religion but an undying science, perfected in Bhakti Yoga; the soul's (citta's) pure state of awareness without the mirror reflection. However, when we visit holy places in India, local guides tell us about Hindus and Buddhists and often give a date at which their religion came into existence. Let us clearly understand that there is no such a thing as *one* "Hindu" system of religion. In India and Nepal for example, we find many "Hindu" belief systems and traditions, such as Shaktism - wherein the faithful worship the energy behind creation in the form of Goddess Durga, also known as Kali. Other people worship the Sun because the Sun maintains them by its heat. Others, realizing the existence of three-dimensional beings beyond the forces of nature, worship Ganesh and Shiva. Further, we come across practices based on the *six philosophies* discussed earlier, such as Karma-mimamsa, *Vedic* rituals, which, by 500 B.C. had become the foremost practice in the Indian subcontinent. During that epoch, the mass of people had taken to this ritualistic lifestyle and justified mass slaughter of animals in the name of *Vedic* sacrifices. As a reaction to such cruelty, another "Hindu" religion emerged: Buddhism, which emphasized non-violence.[25]

The above-mentioned practices, including Buddhism, are to be understood different steps on the Yoga Ladder. As the practitioners progress on the spiritual path, such practices will be abandoned or gradually fade away.[26]

However, we should note that Bhakti Yoga, also known as Vaisnavism (worship of Vishnu or Krishna), is not a "means or step" to a goal. It is the goal. It is transcendental, beyond external designations, and eternally the same. Its Sanskrit designation is "Sanatana Dharma." *Sanatana* means "without beginning or end." Its practice extended and still extends well beyond the geographical borders of India as it is known today, throughout Asia and beyond.[27]

Practitioners are free from temporary identification with the place of birth. They identify with the *atma*. *Ahimsa*, non violence towards all living creatures, is a natural by-product of the practice of Sanatana Dharma.

25 *Science and Religion, The Quest for Synthesis* (BTG Magazine #24-03, 1989) Ravindra Svarupa

26 Buddha himself describes the gradual decline of Buddhism. He said for the first five hundred years it will be possible to follow, then for another five hundred years a shadow of the true teaching will remain, and then it will faint away. See Malcolm David Eckel, *Buddhism: Origins, Beliefs, Practices, Holy Texts, Sacred Places* (New York: Oxford University Press, 2002) for details of this version.

27 From 802 to 1431 A.D., Cambodia—known in its own Sanskrit inscriptions as *Kambuja-desa*—was the mightiest kingdom in Southeast Asia and its rulers build the Angkor Wat temple, the largest temple of Vishnu in the world.

In the name of religion, people deprived from their *atma*-identity take to ritualistic activities, inferior worship, and speculation. When this happens, a restoration effort usually takes place, by higher and divine arrangements.[28]

A restoration might take many centuries. For instance, a country of mostly illiterate citizens does not need to establish universities right away. First, the citizens need to learn the basic alphabet; they require simple, elementary schools. In the same way, Buddha's teachings are preliminary; they are stepping-stones in the restoration that leads to the realization of Bhakti Yoga.

The consciousness of those who habitually eat flesh becomes highly polluted, making it difficult for them to comprehend the difference between the body and the soul. Thus they are unaware of the "Adi-Buddha" dwelling in their own hearts.[29] Often, despite a vegetarian diet, sincere followers of Buddha's teaching of nonviolence are as well unclear about their relationship with that "Adi-Buddha" (the Isvara). Thus they are deprived from the happy experience of Yoga. This is mainly because of inadequate training and can be easily rectified by learning from the original *Vedic* tradition.

When Buddha spread his message, the degraded priestly class opposed him on the strength of scripture, which they had distorted to suit their own aims. To counteract their false propaganda, Buddha rejected the source of their knowledge (the *Vedas*) and did not speak much philosophy. However, at some level of progress, philosophy is needed, lest we remain sentimental followers, unable to logically explain anything.

The way Buddha gained widespread acceptance and respect is remarkable. He convinced people not through philosophy but through his personal influence, by virtue of his exemplary life.[30] Additionally, one should know that unless empowered by the Isvara, nobody can elevate the masses towards spiritual perfection and ultimately to Bhakti Yoga (*krishna-sakti vina nahe tara pravartana*). Gautama Buddha *was*

28 Bhagavad Gita 4.7 purport: "Sometimes He descends personally, and sometimes He sends His bona fide representative in the form of His son, or servant, or Himself in some disguised form."

29 *Adi* literally means the "first" or "primordial;" the Adi Buddha is there before anything was created and he is in the hearts of every creature. Thus, Gautama Buddha, the one who underwent austerities to search out enlightenment, is not that "Adi Buddha" in the heart.

30 On one occasion Buddha said: "Many things I have not explained, because they are not necessary to know. A soldier struck by an arrow does not demand to know who has shot the arrow before having it removed. Similarly, you do not need answer for everything in order to progress." Ranchor Prime, *Prince of Dharma: The illustrated Life of the Buddha* (Novaco, California: Mandala Media, 2002) p. Xii.

empowered. *Vedic* texts, many compiled more than 5000 years ago, predict the appearance of empowered persons and their precise mission, includingBuddha's.[31]

Whether one accepts or rejects Gautama Buddha to be the empowered Buddha predicted in the scriptures, we can safely say that he played a significant part in the spiritual restoration process.[32] In view of the circumstances, Gautama Buddha showed an example that attracted the minds of the degraded people of his time to follow. Bhakti Yoga, the ultimate standard in spiritual perfection, was an "unsuitable subject matter" simply because people were not ready for it, and to elevate them to the top rank of the YogaLadder was not Buddha's mission.

In the course of time, other empowered persons, such as Sankaracarya (the famous teacher of monism already introduced in the second chapter of this book) appeared to again establish *Vedic* thoughts, albeit in a compromised version. In a lifetime spanning only thirty-two years, Sankara replaced Buddhism with *Vedic* teachings. Since then, Buddhism in its different forms has remained in India with a small following of about 0.7% of the whole population. It is noteworthy how in a very short time Sankara managed to turn the followers of Buddha in India into followers of the *Vedic* culture. However, by following Sankara's interpretation of the *Vedas*, the masses did not again succumb to the rituals of animal killing, and to this day vegetarianism prevails in India. According to a study published in 2001, 83% of the population observes vegetarian principles.[33] People did not retrogress because they had achieved higher stages of purity by the influence of such empowered teachers. Buddha was the first to create the favorable condition for this spiritual restoration to take place. After Buddha came Sankara, who paved the way for Ramanujacarya (1017- 1070 A.D.) and Madhvacarya (1239-1319 A.D.), and thereafter Yoga teachings gained momentum. The restoration culminated in 1486 A.D. with the appearance of Sri Caitanya Mahaprabhu and his eternal associates, who established a movement that gradually flooded the entire world with Bhakti

31 The mission of Buddha is predicted in *Srimad-Bhagavatam*, 1.3.24; 2.7.37; 6.8.19; 10.40.22 and 11.4.22 – also in the *Agni Purana*, 16.1-14) Śrīla Jayadeva Gosvāmī, in his *Daśāvatāra-stotra*, writes: *Nindasi yajñavidher ahaha śruti-jātaṁ; sadaya-hṛdaya-darśita-paśu-ghātam; keśava dhṛta-buddha-śarīra jaya jagad-īśa hare*. Srila Prabhupada comments in SB 6.8.19: "The mission of Lord Buddha was to save people from the abominable activity of animal killing and to save the poor animals from being unnecessarily killed. When Pāṣaṇḍīs (offenders) were cheating by killing animals on the plea of sacrificing them in Vedic yajñas, the Lord said, 'If the Vedic injunctions allow animal killing, I do not accept the Vedic principles.' Thus, he actually saved people who acted according to Vedic principles."

32 In the *Lalita-vistara* (a Buddhist text), on page 178, it says, "Gautama Buddha performed tapasya, austerities and penance, at the holy place of the previous Buddha." Some say that the Buddha predicted in the Vedas is that previous Buddha. (see *Rays of the Harmonist*, Vol II No1, Gaudiya Math Press, Navadvipa)

33 Judy W. Patel, *The people of India: Their Religion, Culture and Way of Being* (New York: The Falmut Educational Trust. 2001) p.212

Yoga - as is evident today. In 1966, when A. C. Bhaktivedanta Swami Prabhupada began translating the wealth of Bhakti Yoga texts into the English language, the movement went far beyond the borders of India and reached all five continents, where anyone, including you, dear reader, can get in touch with that spiritual wealth, become an empowered person, and enter the circle of associates of the Isvara. Caitanya Mahaprabhu's contribution is a benediction from the spiritual plane, a special boon to attain the topmost enlightenment in a degraded era.

In the next section I examine the development and spread of Buddhism after Buddha's departure. By so doing I hope to help the reader relinquish any lingering doubt as to the topmost value of Bhakti Yoga, the practice of which softens the heart and makes one eligible to receive mercy. Traces of this significant "mercy-feature" in spiritual practice can be found in some later version of Buddhism, albeit without a profound insight regarding the complete process. Receiving mercy is certainly an integral part of "Pure Land Buddhism."[34] Mercy means a divine intervention that causes a change of *citta* (desire).

After the demise of Gautama Buddha, around 483 B.C., confusion arose among his followers. Two camps formed, viz. the Theravada (Hinayana) and the Mahayana. The Theravada brand of Buddhism, commonly found in Sri Lanka, Cambodia, Myanmar, and Thailand, is the conservative monastic lifestyle shown by the Buddha. In China, Japan, Korea, and Vietnam we generally find the Mahayana school, whose more liberal approach to the Buddha's way of life, aims to give all sentient beings a chance for liberation. Schools of Buddhism multiplied. For example, Nagarjuna, a philosopher and teacher of Buddhism in the second century A.D., established that nothing exists and reality, if properly perceived, is simply a void or emptiness (*sunyata*). His teachings became the first branch of Mahayana with a systematic philosophy, holding a conclusion close to the one that Sankara later on propounded.[35] In later chapters we discuss how one is unable to reach the spiritual platform by negative abstraction.[36] Thus, Nagarjuna's conclusion largely reflects his

---

34 This version of Buddhism is well known in Taiwan. The teaching says that there is a spiritual paradise called *Sukhavati*. By chanting the name "Amitabha," particularly at the time of death, one will attain this abode. In this version of Buddhism, success in spiritual perfection depends not only on one's own effort: one attains help from outside, if one is humble enough to ask for it. For more information on it and its connection to Bhakti Yoga, see Tamal Krishna Goswami's *A funny thing happened on the way to Nirvana: When the Path of Vaisnava-Bhakti crossed Amitabha's Pure Land*, in *A Hare Krishna at Southern Methodist University, Collected Essays 1995-1997* (Dallas, Texas, Pundits Press, 1998)

35 Sankara interpreted the *Upanishads - Vedic* thought of no interest to the followers of Buddha–in a way that these followers could appreciate, which led to the acceptance of Vedic texts and the restoration of the original *Vedic* culture.

36 The Bhagavad-gita recommends a mood of humility and service to a teacher situated on the top rank of the Yoga Ladder (a Bhakti Yoga guru) for one who desires to progress. (Bg. 4.34)

own condition and is unlikely to be what Gautama Buddha originally shared with his followers. Whatever the case might be, the philosophies of Nagarjuna and Sankara do not stand scrutiny (see Appendix Four).

Other branches, such as Yogachara, headed by a monk called Asanga in the fourth century A.D., blended Astanga-Yoga practices into their practices, Asanga differed from Nagarjuna in establishing that consciousness (*atma*) consists of eternal individuality.[37] Vajrayana, "the diamond vehicle," is still another form of Buddhism. It employs mysticism and magic, thereby accepting a host of celestial beings. This form of Buddhism is most popular in Bengal and Tibet, but people also practice it in Mongolia, Sikkim, and Nepal. In its Tibetan form, the ideal of the "Bodhisattva Buddha" is the Dalai Lama, and people show respect to him as the one who incarnated to guide them, which indicates that they accept the permanent nature of the atma.

These are some of the earliest forms of Buddhism. Many more appeared in due course of time, such as Zen in China and Japan[38], and each one believes that it conveys Buddha's teaching more accurately than the other. Paradoxically, many of these teachers and followers do not shun the eating of animals. Can they still claim to follow Buddha's path? The host of different and sometimes even opposing views - not about trivial matters but about fundamental issues like reincarnation and the identity of Buddha - they hold makes one wonder if such persons are truly knowledgeable and if their practice can really lead them to enlightenment? I leave it up to the reader to decide.

Enlightenment is not a vague concept. From the Bhagavad-gita we understand that enlightenment is the attainment of pure consciousness - the prerequisite awareness for acting in Bhakti Yoga.[39] Patanjali Muni, Gautama Buddha, and Sankara alike were exceptional personalities situated on that pure platform (Brahman). They had their allotted missions and accomplished them. We, individual souls, can take inspiration from their example in order to be able to carry out our life's mission, regardless of obstacles and misconceptions. We

---

37 In due course, teachers of Yogachara also took to the view that even individual consciousness is an illusion, thereby joining the ranks of the *sunyatas*.

38 The word "Zen" comes from the Chinese word "Chan," derived from the Sanskrit "Dhyana, meaning "meditation" or "concentration." The first teacher was the Chinese Master Yang-chi Fang Hoi. Zen has gained much popularity amongst Westerners, because of its simple practice and abstract philosophy that is inexpressible, beyond reason and logic.

39 Bg 18.54 *brahma bhuta prasanatma*... "One who is thus transcendentally situated at once realizes the Supreme Brahman and becomes fully joyful. He never laments or desires to have anything. He is equally disposed toward every living entity. In that state he attains pure devotional service to Me."

should be progressive and not remain stuck on any step of the Yoga Ladder until we reach the top - the attainment of complete purity, which manifests as selfless love for Krishna. Let us make full use of our pilgrimage. Let us, by the influence of the holy atmosphere and holy association in holy places, take inspiration and knowledge from the Adi-Buddha within the heart,[40] happily walk the path of Bhakti Yoga, and regain our original identity.

Assembled at Bodhgaya

40 Bg 10.10 *dadami buddhi-yogam tam...* from within I give them intelligence *(buddhi-yoga)*

CHAPTER SEVEN

OPTING FOR - The Direct Path

The ancient Yoga culture formerly practiced by great kings and handed down to their citizens does not seem to be relevant in the contemporary world. Most governments around the world have established secularism.[41] State-run educational institutes normally teach nothing about spiritual life. In some regions, as a reaction to materialism, one observes various brands of fanatical fundamentalism. The majority of people are ignorant of how to make spiritual progress. On my travels I frequently speak to taxi drivers to get some understanding of what the common person in that particular country does. The general pattern is working from morning till night, ending the day with much needed relaxation in the shape of alcohol, TV, and sex. Looking at this type of life pattern from the Yoga perspective, we see the modes of passion and ignorance in action.

As already pointed out, there are reasons for the prominence of ignorance in the modern world and I mentioned the popularity of countless bogus teachers and self-proclaimed spiritual mentors. Frankly speaking, things that go on in today's world in the name of spirituality are largely misunderstandings with no clear concept of an Absolute Truth or Yoga. The world we live in could be a peaceful place, but due to the prominence of *tama guna* (ignorance), it has now become a difficult place in which many people have to struggle just to survive.

On a more positive note, we have increased our global awareness, primarily about ecological and environmental problems. People take more interest in alternative thinking and desire peace of mind that often leads them to spiritualism. This trend, commonly called "new age," espouses a broad range of practices. Yoga teachings are part of that scene. Bhaktivedanta Swami Prabhupada

41 secularism (sek'yuh luh riz uhm) n. > the view that public education and other matters of civil policy should be conducted without the influence of spiritual beliefs (Webster's Dictonary)

explains that in such circles it is fashionable to say that whatever one does or whatever path one follows is all right. If one can do anything and call it a path, then what is the meaning of a teacher? A particular phenomenon of our modern times is that many persons misconceive spiritual life as a kind of ongoing search for the Truth. Searching for anything implies that you know what you are looking for, likely something you have lost. So one should have at least some basic ideas of what one is looking for, otherwise, what is the purpose of searching? There should be standard questions, such as "who am I?" and "what is the purpose of existence?" When one comes across clear answers and is shown how to apply such answers into real life, one should accept these answers. However, many persons profess liberalism and open-mindedness and at the same time they are very much opposed to accepting authorities that teach them conclusive spiritual knowledge. Making a show of tolerance towards all kinds of even mistaken ideas and promoting an attitude of being non-judgmental, they nevertheless become very intolerant of the absolute statements made in the Bhagavad-gita and similar works. They sometimes teach that one does not need a teacher for spiritual progress, which is obviously contradictory to their own activities. If there is no need for teachers, then why are they writing? Actually, for the betterment of the world, we badly need qualified teachers to guide the ignorant.

But how practical is Yoga? Can I do it? We have already seen that the path to Samadhi through the eightfold system is tough. Each of the eight steps has to be strictly followed and perfected. Yoga is a science, so one has to follow the procedure exactly to get the result. For example, pranayama, control of the breath, means that ultimately the Yogi comes to the point of almost stopping his breathing. Only then can he take the next step, withdrawing the senses from all material engagements. We can see from this example why authentic Yoga teachers say that for the present age we should not waste our time even trying. If one could follow the practices perfectly, the results would definitely come. But the difficulty is that the practices are very hard to master.

Bhakti Yoga, however, is simple and direct, and it is the path recommended by the sages of yore for our present age. One need not go through the preliminary stages of mechanically trying to subdue the mind and senses by long, difficult exercises in sitting, breathing, sensory discipline, and so on. Instead, one comes directly to the highest stage - samadhi, constant meditation on the Supreme Absolute - by, for example, chanting the transcendental Names of the Absolute.

Patanjali points towards this practice in YS 2.45, where he says that one attains perfect samadhi simply by meditating on and surrendering to the Isvara (*samadhi-siddhir isvarapranidhanat*). Patanjali earlier said (YS 1.24-26):

klesa-karma-vipakasayair aparamasnah purusa-visesa isvarah; tatra niratisayaṁ sarvajnya-bijam; sa tu purvesam api guru kalenanavacchedat. "Isvara (the Supreme) is a certain person who is untouched by suffering, karma, destiny, or calamity. He knows everything. Because He is untouched by time, He is the master of all." In the direct Bhakti Yoga process one does not need to undergo all the disciplines of the eightfold process step by step before one can attain this perfection. Patanjali might not be explicitly stressing Bhakti Yoga in his teachings, but he certainly indicates that we should ultimately focus our attention on the Isvara. Having accepted that the goal is to focus our attention on the Isvara, why not, then, directly engage in the Bhakti Yoga process? Attention comes as an effect of attraction and loving feelings. We are attracted by beauty, greatness, wisdom, and so on and pay full attention to them when they are displayed. Especially beauty is attractive and implies form, in the case of the Absolute Truth, spiritual form. This form is known as Krishna.

The principal difficulty of many so-called spiritual teachers is the refusal to accept the eternal complete spiritual form of the Absolute Truth. They do not know that, *om purnam adam purnam idam*...(Isopanishad, Invocation). The meaning of this verse is that although everything emanates from the Absolute Truth, He nevertheless does not diminish. We emanate from and belong to the whole, yet we are not the whole; we are particles of it. (Fig. 9) Therefore we should act in this world in the mood of humble service to the whole, as a part of a machine functions for the whole machine. If, however, we act with selfish interests and not as intended, for the purpose of the whole, we implicate ourselves in "the law of Karma."[42]

Fig. 9: The Absolute Truth is compared to the sun, and the living entities to sunshine. (Bg. 18.78 p)

On the other hand, by the practice of Bhakti Yoga, our Karma (action) in this world turns into

42 "The law of Karma": Every action has an equal opposite reaction, gross and subtle as explained in relation to the influence of the gunas on our "*citta*" and our *prarabdha-karma.* See Chapter Three.

action of purification, as explained in Chapter Five, and one moves upward on the "Yoga Ladder." With purified minds in the quality of goodness, one becomes happy and one is no longer aggressive towards any other being. As one progresses, selfishness in the form of greed and envy totally disappears from the awareness (*citta*), and gives way to selfless love (*prema*).

The practice of Bhakti Yoga will affect the condition of life in this world. In the next chapter, we look at the working of "the law of Karma" and the consequences of ignoring it.

Serene Walk alongside Yamuna

CHAPTER EIGHT

ABIDING BY - The Law of Karma

In the 1960s the term Karma became a popular word in American hip jargon - a word similar to *fate*: you can't do anything about it. But this is a misconception. Factually, Karma is an unbreakable law of nature that awards happiness and suffering to all living beings according to their pious or sinful acts. Ultimately, there is no good Karma, because even so-called good Karma will force one to accept another material body to stay in the cycle of birth, disease, old age, and death. Patanjali is well aware of the law of Karma. For example he says in YS 3.18 that one who has attained enlightenment is able to know the consequences of his actions, and thus he has the power to calculate correctly the exact length of his life. The law of Karma is not imaginary, but to be able to see it working requires some training. It is a change of paradigm. Actions have reactions, and not knowing how to act does not free one from the consequences. The following event illustrates this concept:

"The UN says that at least 340,000 Somalis have fled their capital, Mogadishu, in the recent weeks of fighting there. Thousands more are trapped along the frontlines inside the city, under fire, packed in with rotting corpses, and unable to find a way out. Most of the displaced civilians are encamped on Mogadishu's outskirts, where the scenes are medieval. People lack water, food and shelter. Cholera has broken out. The sick sometimes have to pay rent even to sit in the shade of trees. Things will get worse with the rains, which have started. Aid agencies say people will soon start dying in large numbers". (Thursday April 26th, 2007)[43]

What is happening here? At the political level it has already been analyzed. But journalists and news agencies, unconcerned with the natural laws of action and reaction, do not realize that in Somalia and other places a devastating truth is being acted out: the law of Karma.

---

43 http://www.economist.com/world/africa/displaystory.cfm?story_id=9090247

A good number of people accept that what happens to them in life is handled by an invisible destiny. They know that to take birth in a wealthy family, or to get the chance to be well-educated, or to have a beautiful physique, is not accidental. They sense an arrangement behind all these situations, and they know it stems from good deeds of the past. Being in this world means to reap the results of past activities and to engage in new activities, which means that a fresh pile of bad Karma accumulates whenever one endeavors for one's own benefit. Everyone is active but mostly not for the benefit of others: "What's in it for me?" we ask. But many people do not know that what is done for one's personal interest brings about a reaction, good for good and bad for bad. Therefore, practically and simultaneously, we keep piling up new shares and ripping off past shares of Karma.

Often the reactions are ghastly, like in Somalia - the result of accumulated unlawful activities. At a given point in time, the reactions strike - severely. By the arrangement of the law of nature, when members of a society receive the reactions for their misdeeds, they may themselves become the tools to carry out those reactions. At such times, their normal ability to make proper choices becomes disabled, and they helplessly respond to the dictates of their environment, acting like chased animals. Bereft of their spiritual or intellectual acumen, their lower instincts triggered by anxiety, fear, and hate, they operate solely on carnal impulses, pouncing on each other like beasts, torturing, raping, and killing, often in a manner worse than a beast would. In this way, they become instruments to act out the law of Karma, enforcing the reactions of past misdeeds on each other.

Hence, Afghanistan and Iraq, Somalia and Darfur, and in the past Rwanda, Cambodia, two World Wars, and so on. All that happens, has happened, and will happen in the future, is simply the enactment of the law of Karma - in the form of wars, cataclysms, epidemics, diseases, accidents, legal tribulations, and so on.

There are compelling reasons why ancient scriptures such as the Vedas consider animal killing, intoxication, and unregulated sex to be improper. The universal codes of righteousness have been given, and to break them causes bad reactions. We all know that tax evasion is punishable by law, and what to speak of violent and unethical acts? Why should we think that going against the universal laws won't bring reactions? The karmic toll accumulates, and we then pay through experiencing calamities, or perhaps even taking birth in a war torn environment.

Fighting for natural resources, we unleash upon humanity global heating with changing weather patterns and political unrest - these days one doesn't have to be a certified paranoid to fear the worst. Some might conclude that they should pray for better times and might be hopeful that they will be protected from miseries. But the laws of nature are not something one can bargain with. Mankind has constantly acted in irresponsible ways, and when the reactions in the forms of war, famine, and so many other natural disturbances come, they pray that these things should not take place. Such matters are not resolved so simply. Consider a criminal: he commits a theft, and when he is captured by the police force, he pleads for his punishment to be waived.

That is not likely to happen. In the same manner, people are engaged in many forbidden activities, and by nature's law there must be a reaction. Nature is not an order supplier. Nature is an order executer. When millions of defenseless animals and millions of human embryos are slaughtered every year, the killers and their accomplices have to bear heavy karmic reactions. Nature arranges for this to occur. This is not to say that Karma cannot be changed. We can change our actions and thus neutralize the reactions. That is the power of Bhakti (Bg 18.66)[44]. There is no point in wishfully talking of peace and mercy until one first agrees to change one's actions. Therefore one should learn how the phenomenal world works and what one is supposed to do. The Bhagavad-gita, the original discourse on Yoga and Karma, explains all these aspects very clearly. The impetus to act for our own selfish material interests has to be transferred to act for the satisfaction of the Isvara. We must act in Bhakti Yoga and awaken to the higher taste of spiritual activities. Merely by mundane welfare activities one cannot stop karmic reactions. Nor can that be stopped by the activities recommended in the *Vedas* to get good Karma: Good Karma does not counter bad Karma; both effects will have to be experienced in due course of time. Hence one can observe people who are extremely bad but enjoy great prosperity and so-called good persons undergoing intense misery.

The leaders of the world may hope for a world government united by an enlightened ideology that will put an end to all wars and suffering. Such an ideology has to include the understanding of the law of Karma. In the past and at present the bloodshed caused by fighting groups is mainly due to a lack of understanding about the law of Karma. The majority of people are breaking this universal law and are thus accountable. It is alarming to notice climatic changes due to global warming and frightening to see the global stockpile of nuclear weapons become larger and more deadly. It is only a question of time before we are faced with a disaster. The stringent law of Karma leaves no doubt about it - unless we give up our selfish endeavors and mentality and act only for the

44 *sarva-pāpebhyo mokṣayiṣyāmi* - freedom from all sinful reactions through Bhakti Yoga.

ultimate benefit of all. As we have seen, international diplomacy is not the solution. What the world needs is saintly leadership, leaders who have knowledge of Yoga, of the law of Karma, and who understand how to perform actions that do not bring about material reactions. Until we learn this, we will go on hearing shattering reports about disasters of every kind and keep on wondering how these things are taking place and why nobody is able to prevent them from happening.

How can one be controlled by Karma through the medium of nature (*gunas*) and still believe that one is entirely free and independent? This question is the topic of our next Chapter.

Free to sing & dance

CHAPTER NINE

CHOOSING - Albeit with Limited Freedom

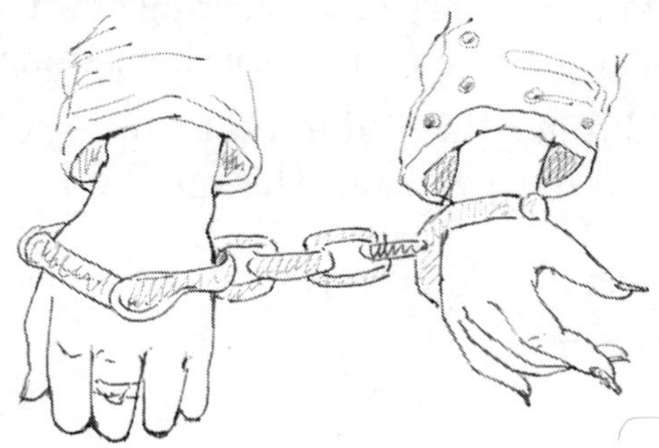

We pointed out in the Introduction that Patanjali's teachings will not make much sense when stripped of the concepts of Karma, the soul, and reincarnation, The concept of reincarnation in particular is an implicit idea in the entire Yoga science. This is evident from YS 4.10 which declares that there is no beginning (*anaditvam*) to life. YS 4, text 8, states that the effects of mental deposits made in previous lives create a certain type of bodily and mental condition, as well as an environment to act upon - in other words what we now are. Throughout the teachings of Patanjali, the concept of Karma and reincarnation is taken for granted.

Reincarnation is a very important science. The current trend of interest in reincarnation is good, provided it leads to the right understanding. However, inaccurate and fanciful literatures on the subject often repel serious thinkers from considering it further. Knowledge about reincarnation should be properly studied through the Bhagavad-gita and other Yoga teachings, not through whimsical theories and persons lacking in authorized references.

Of course, we are free to choose between knowledge and ignorance. Or are we? Do we have our own free will to decide whom we want to believe and to what extent we want to apply ourselves to any type of spiritual practice? This is an important question because the answer will tell us whether we are victims of our destiny - and therefore innocent - or not.

As shown in Chapter Three, Fig. 7, we are absorbed in the mirror reflection. In fact, we, the person (the *atma*), are not truly aware of what we do, because in illusion we think we are that reflection (*ahankara*). In fact, it seems that the real person does not do anything; absorbed in the excitements of the external world, he is like a mad person. Why then should the law of Karma hold him responsible for his deeds?

Yoga knowledge holds that the real person (*atma*), not the mind or body, is the eternal individual, and that he has no factual connection with the ever mutable material energy (*asango 'yam purusah*). We have some experience of this concept because we retain the same sense of identity throughout one life experience. I'm always "I," despite my body having changed from childhood to old age, along with the concomitant changes of thoughts. Yoga teaches that we have no connection with this world of matter. Somehow or other we are attached to it, and we have forgotten our original, real, identity and residence altogether. Hence the question: Is the *atma* merely an observer and not an actor? Is the soul - which takes on different types of bodies in different species - given any freedom to decide what he wants? Or is he just tossed around like an unmanned boat on the sea, with no means to change direction? How much freedom and independence has that individual soul? And to what extend is one compelled to act by the forces of nature?

"Tiny free will" is Prabhupada's phrase to solve the puzzle. We have tiny free will, and we exercise it. The working of the material energy influences our decision-making capacity, but whereas animals and other lower forms, which have much less evolved consciousness, are mostly programmed by instinct, we humans also make conscious choices, and consequently we are responsible for those decisions. In other words, humans get karmic reactions and animals don't. True, animals can be trained and taught tricks which break their normal behavior (not to bark, or to walk, or whatever). However, evolved consciousness and the choice-making capacity are unique features of the soul in the human form. Humans, therefore, are not simply ruled by the modes of nature. Choosing to practice Bhakti Yoga, for example, is not induced by the dictates of material nature; somehow, the person gets some awareness of his factual position and decides to pursue a way of life that leads to increased awareness and ultimate freedom from the forces of material nature.

The balance between free will and conditioning by the material energy is something like an animal on a leash. Even on a leash, the animal experiences some kind of freedom when walking in the garden, but factually he is obliged to follow the path the master chooses. Similarly, we are bound to act in accordance with the

specific type of body and character we have acquired in previous lives, and we only imagine that we are doing whatever we do because we want it.[45] In reality, our senses and mind dictate to us in a way that limits our true freedom. Depending on how good we are at controlling our mind and senses by a regulated life style, we progress to the mode of goodness, within which we receive more freedom, because we have earned it and will likely use it wisely; ignorance means less freedom, more restriction, "a shorter leash." Therefore, while we are on a leash of some kind, we simultaneously have some modest mobility, lesser or greater, depending upon our association with the different modes. How the living entity (*atma)* is enslaved in the tight grip of material nature and at the same time has some kind of choice and activity can be compared to the attempt of a small boy to lift a weight he has just seen his father lift. The boy first desires to lift the weight and then tries. He cannot possibly succeed, but his father sees his small son's desire, stands above him, and out of affection does the actual lifting. Thus the father has actually lifted the weight, but he cannot be considered the only lifter. Unless the desire had been expressed and the attempt made by the child, the father would not have helped and the weight would not have been lifted. The *atma* is therefore not a mere neutral observer (inactive); he is actively involved but not the only cause; it desires and attempts, and nature acts.

How then is material nature acting? What is that "father" who links the eternal non-material (*atma*) with the changing material? It is the Isvara (*Paramatma*). Matter is inert and needs the touch of spirit. Everything in the material world is

45 Refer to Fig. 8 in Chapter Three: The person (*atma*) is situated on a horse chariot

moving because of the presence of the *atma* and the Isvara, (Bg 18.13-17). Some people teach that one should meditate on the thought: "It is because of me that the sun rises and the wind blows," but such persons are bewildered. True, we are spirit and not matter (*aham brahmasmi*), but we are *part* of the whole, not *the* whole. In other words, we are not the Paramatma, the One who oversees and sanctions all the living being's specific karmic results. We are subordinate to Him and subjected to the law of Karma.

We explained in Chapter Four that by the eightfold Yoga practice (Astanga-Yoga) one attains to the stage of Samadhi wherein one is perfectly united with the Isvara in a mood of service and subordination. Hence, to always think of the Isvara is the perfection of Yoga. How this is done, by the practice of Bhakti Yoga, is explained in the Bhagavad-gita: "One should meditate upon the Supreme Person as the One who knows everything, as He who is the oldest, who is the controller, who is smaller than the smallest, who is the maintainer of everything, who is beyond all material conception, who is inconceivable, and who is always a person. He is luminous like the sun, and He is transcendental, beyond this material nature." (Bg 8.9)

On the other hand, when the living entity, ignorant of and uninterested in his eternal relationship with the Isvara, chooses to be an independent enjoyer, he is welded to material nature and placed under its control. In ignorance, he then considers himself entirely independent, although in reality he is not at all free. Still, he is responsible for his own destiny. Human beings are accountable for all their actions because it is they who express the desire, they who make the attempt, and they who want to enjoy the fruit of their actions.[46]

We hope this little study enables the reader to gain a better perspective and understanding of what life is all about and of the ignorant condition most of us are in. The next Chapter takes us further into the discussion of knowledge and ignorance. As already pointed out, unless we get all the concepts right (paradigm changes) we will not be able to wholeheartedly dive into the ocean of Bhakti Yoga.

Because the topic of proper perspective (paradigm) is most significant for spiritual progress, we discuss in detail next what the factors are that make one reason in favor of, or against any type of understanding. In other words, what causes one to "know"?

46 Parts of this chapter are adapted from *Surrender unto Me*, Bhurijana dasa (see Bibliography)

CHAPTER TEN

DISCARDING - Old Paradigms

We tend to think in terms of what our contemporaries think and say. To begin with, most of us get educated by what some people have decided to classify as knowledge. So we end up thinking in identical ways. We seldom pause to consider seriously how and why we have come to think the way we think. Since in this day and age we are in a different frame of mind than that of people in previous ages, we need to be aware of that difference, so that we can better understand yogic knowledge. We are so close to what we routinely do and think that we are unable to have a broad perspective on our lives and on the events that occur around us - we see trees but not the forest that comprises them. Yoga knowledge represents the broadest possible view.

Let us admit that our present mindset is inadequate to enter Patanjali's teachings. Consider for example, a student of classical Chinese literature or Shakespeare. Such a student is required to be familiar with the values and norms of that time in order to understand the literature. Similarly, we need to adjust our thinking, our mindset, in order to enter the yogic teachings. The modern term for mindset is *paradigm*, and the understanding of what paradigms are is very well documented in a significant study about the history of science, "The Structure of Scientific Revolutions", by Thomas Kuhn.[47] The principles of his findings apply to scientific knowledge as well as to knowledge in any other field.

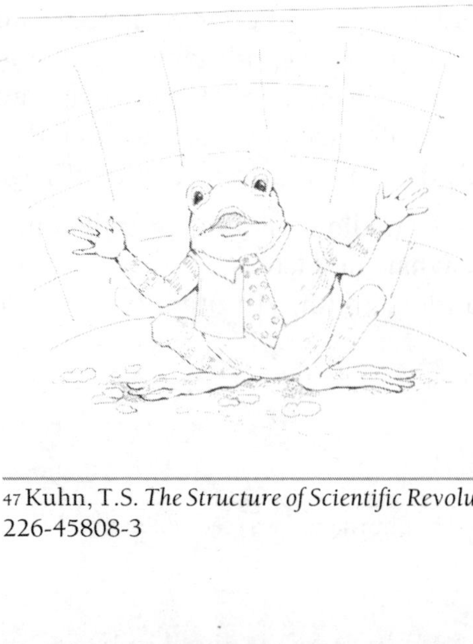

47 Kuhn, T.S. *The Structure of Scientific Revolutions*. Chicago: University of Chicago Press, 1962. ISBN 0-226-45808-3

Kuhn explains how paradigms determine the fundamentals by which we view the world. Paradigms determine what we can and cannot acknowledge, so that although one may see, one does not recognize. The usual tendency is to compare everything with one's own predetermined standards. For example, a frog living in a well cannot even begin to conceptualize the size of an ocean; thus, when informed of the greatness of the ocean, the frog understands it as being a slightly larger version of its well. As such, we tend to have certain pre-conceived convictions, and hence we find it difficult to accept how reality could actually be different from our pre-conceived ideas.

We discussed in Chapter Three how the mind works: the mind is influenced by the gunas we associate with. We associate with the gunas because we want to enjoy matter, although as spiritual beings we are not meant to do so. The example of a monkey trying to grab a banana inside a pot illustrates the point of our bondage with matter. The pot has an opening just big enough for the monkey to insert and withdraw his empty hand. But when the monkey holds the banana in his fist, the size of his fist is enlarged and he cannot withdraw his hand from the pot. Out of intense greed to enjoy the banana, the monkey won't let go of it, and thus he is trapped. Similarly, we souls are caught and trapped by the modes of material nature, because we try to hold on to the material energy for enjoyment. In this world, the material energy causes ordinary persons to forget their essential nature and to identify with the thoughts that arise within their minds in connection with the various forms and objects of this world. Yoga aims at freedom from such impressions, which are stored in the mind from many lifetimes.

Nevertheless, thinking, feeling and willing are part of our spiritual nature too. Thus we should employ these faculties on the spiritual platform, which is what Bhakti Yoga is about. As long as we do not reach that pure platform, we will remain in the grip of material ideas (paradigms), which are all pervasive and instinctive within any given culture. People tend to surround themselves with associates who hold identical paradigms, and in this way they reinforce their views. A Chinese person of our generation thinks the way most other people think in China. But if that very same person had been raised in Japan and imbibed that cultural paradigm instead, he would be thinking the Japanese way. And if that same person could travel back in time to the age of Yoga culture, he would still be the same person, but his conceptions and convictions would be different.

One might say that nowadays we base our knowledge on science and that science has progressed to the extent that we can understand a lot more things than before about this world. We might thus conclude that our present paradigms are more correct than the previous ones. Is this really so? Are scientists, who are human and frail, sufficiently objective and in a position to know things properly?

The question for an inquisitive mind is, how can anyone be sure that he has the correct view of things? How can anyone be confident that his paradigm and yardstick are the real thing? Each individual's judgments are founded on paradigms and biased subjectivity, and scientists are not excluded from this predicament. To be fair, we also have to ask whether Patanjali's views and the *Vedas* are correct, especially because their thinking is diametrically opposed to the conventional contemporary view.

For the time being, suffice to say that in order to understand the teachings expounded by Patanjali, it is necessary to understand how we are presently in the grip of paradigms. We should therefore agree to take a step back and at least theoretically accept Patanjali's version of the existence of the soul and the concomitant subordinate role of the body in which it dwells. For Patanjali holds that matter exists for the soul's sake, taking it for granted that the student believes in the existence of the soul. Hence, he does not go into attempting to prove that which in his days was acknowledged as a fact. According to him, the real "Experiencer" and "Knower" is the soul, and not even the material mind. This means that the mind, the thinking principle, while higher and more subtle than the body, is yet only an instrument used by the soul to gain experience. We pointed out earlier how Patanjali devotes much attention to the mind, and how the mind is the cause of bondage and also the cause of release from bondage. (Bg 6.5) The pure soul decided to be bound to matter and experience itself as the body: "I am the body;" but the embodied soul can progress and come to realize that "I am the soul within the body." Thus a new way of life opens up.

The paradigm of modern science leaves no room for the views expressed by Patanjali. But for the sake of progressing in the Yoga science we should for now, at least hypothetically, accept the concepts. Only then can we apply ourselves with full attention to the practices Patanjali teaches, gain access to new realizations, and thus change to a new paradigm. That new paradigm might turn out to be much more convincing than the paradigms endorsed by so-called science.

Honest scientists do admit that they have not yet come to understand what the ultimate truth is. How do we explain the coming into existence of the highly complex functions of a single micro-organism? The answers given by today's scientists are not final. Thomas Kuhn, in "The Structure of Scientific Revolutions," points out that science undergoes periodic revolutions. When a paradigm is well established and routine work goes on within its parameters, we have "normal science." The paradigm endures because it has explained many things and pointed the way for further research; it has brought intelligible order into the world and it promises to keep on doing so. Therefore, a few anomalies here and there should not bother anyone too much; hence they're put aside to deal with later - and usually forgotten.

However, if gradually the anomalies accumulate so much that they can no longer be ignored, science enters a period of crisis. At that point, someone may come up with a new and radically different method of scientific approach, something that, theoretically speaking, starts afresh. It accounts for the anomalous material and sets research off in an entirely new direction. Quite often an outsider, someone free from the mindset of normal science, provides the new paradigm. For example, John Dalton, who was not a chemist but a meteorologist, proposed the atomic theory.[48]

What is presented now as facts might turn out to be wrong later. Scientific concepts are basically paradigms, many of them represented by individuals who have much to lose if proved wrong. Recently two scientists have published a book entitled "Forbidden Archeology," which points out many anomalies in science.[49] After researching original reports of excavations and looked at the way anomalies in the evidence for human evolutions have been dealt with, the two scientists noticed that the anomaly collection was surprisingly large. Rocks and fossils records show

Fig. 10: Has modern man come to understand his origin?

48 Dalton John> 1766-1844 (Webster's)

49 http://www.forbiddenarcheology.com/

that humans have co-existed for millions of years with apes and other creatures. It was clear from the handling of the findings that there is a double-standard for accepting data: what appears to agree with a conceived theory is easily accepted, and what appears as a contradiction is subject to a more intense level of doubt. If the same standards of unambiguity were applied to all the data, we would arrive at a different conclusion.

The formidable defense mechanism of modern science to keep anomalies from interfering with their evolutionary paradigm shows that the stakes are very high. The evolutionary paradigm puts a frame around people's lives; it tells them who they are, how the world came into being, and how they got there in the first place. If the theory of evolution is abandoned or discredited, people are going to say, "Here I am, here you are, here's this world around us - and I have no idea of how I, or you, or this civilization, or this world got here." To ask these questions is an important aspect of the Yoga study.

Undoubtedly, most of us think we do know and that our understanding is based on valid facts. However, it is not so simple. There is a saying that "a person convinced against his will is of the same opinion still." My desires and expectations dictate my convictions. Have you ever wondered why people end up in court to solve their disagreements? Each party thinks that he is right. But unless I am completely without selfish motives, I will not be able to verify what is correct. Paradigms dictate. But if one learns how to distance oneself from one's situation and look at one's surroundings through a different paradigm, one suddenly discovers facts one was unable to see before. We have to do some serious digging in order to get down to the root, because even what gets acknowledged or recognized as a fact, even the very criteria of what constitutes a fact, are often determined by a paradigm. A fresh paradigm lights up a whole, new world. Knowledge is not a simple thing - it depends on what we want, what we love, and what our hopes and fears are. To get real knowledge we must learn to love the right things, to hope and fear the right things. *Sattvat sanjayate jnanam*... knowledge depends upon the mode of goodness, says the Bhagavad-gita (14.17). The many persons that come up with various doctrines to explain the origin of this world or "The Art of Living"[50] in this world are more often than not subjected to the influence of the modes of material nature, and by it to a resultant particular

50 An organization with people cultivating the mode of goodness is "The Art of Living," established in 1981 by Sri Sri Ravishankara. He made himself a name as a spiritual and humanitarian leader. He envisions a violence-free, stress-free society through the reawakening of human values. But for his vision to succeed, the principles of the Bhagavad-gita will have to be applied without interpretation. Depending on his ability to do so, his followers will or will not become freed from selfishness."

paradigm. Even though goodness is also limiting, it is a necessary condition for receiving perfect knowledge.

To know the factual position of the living entities and to determine what proper actions are, we have to get knowledge from a source free from the influence of matter. Repeating those teachings without adding our own interpretation would make our teaching correct, even though we might still be influenced by the modes. The Bhagavad-gita states that such knowledge is indeed available and is given to mankind at different times (Bg.4.7).

Thomas Kuhn notes that in science, an old paradigm is left behind only when there is a new, more satisfactory one to replace it. An understanding of Bhakti Yoga as given in the Bhagavad-gita provides this satisfactory paradigm. We should be convinced that Yoga can bring about a revolution in our world view. Read on... and enter into this fresh new view.

A traditional Pilgrimage

CHAPTER ELEVEN

DIVERTING FROM - The Direct Path

Years ago, before I understood humankind's dilemma, I tried at times to do good for others - offering my working capacity without remuneration; giving away possessions. I also gave what I considered to be good advice with regard to eating vegetarian food or living a natural, simple life. Such deeds made me feel happy and a little detached from this world. In essence, I was quite aware of the general state of ignorance (including my own) that governed people's lives, and I felt sorry about it, desiring improvement for them as well as for myself. As a result of such desires it so happened that I came in contact with Bhakti Yogis. That ended my mundane service to humanity, and my real fortune began. Hearing the Yoga philosophy from factually learned persons helped me to at least theoretically understand that I was not my body but an eternal, spiritual being, *atma*.

Thinking over this period of my life, I realize that because of the sincerity of my search and the willingness to accept whatever direction my life would take as a result of that search, the Isvara helped me from within to understand where to find the genuine truth. I had read different books, but I found Prabhupada's explanations of the Bhagavad-gita to be matchless. It is clear to me that Bhakti Yoga is the ultimate goal of knowledge, and therefore I can easily identify the errors and misconceptions people teach in the name of spirituality. For example, while introducing a commercialized idea of meditation, some teachers put forward the notion that a Mantra is a word, or sounds, that have no particular meaning. Actually, as explained by Patanjali, Mantra meditation refers to the process of purifying the mind by absorption in the sound vibration of the Isvara's holy Name. His Names are identical with Himself, and by chanting them we enter into blissful, purifying union with Him. This cannot be achieved by simply repeating any meaningless sound.

In China, more and more books on Yoga and spirituality are on the market. Be wary, dear reader; the teachings contained in most of these books are plainly wrong, taught as they are by unqualified persons who, by their culture and education, know a little something about Yoga. They fabricate the rest by using their brains and imagination, as the following example will illustrate: "The Absolute is not a person (*Purusha*), it is an experience. The vision, the experience one has of the universe, of existence, after the dissolution of the ego-center, when the 'I' disappears, what remains is 'Love.' When the walls surrounding ego crumble, what remains, is Love. And that itself is also the Absolute. Hence, one cannot know the Absolute but one can become that Absolute."[51] The underlying thought here is the mistaken notion that because the Absolute expanded Himself and became matter - and the many individual living entities (*atmas*) - He therefore could no longer exist, just as a large piece of paper no longer exists once it has been torn into little pieces. According to such an idea, matter and the living entities make up the Absolute. This is the underlying wrong idea of the person quoted above; and therefore he concludes that one can become Him (the Absolute) (*tat tvam asi* - you are that).

The person quoted is notorious for indulging in sex with his students. In fact, some say he died of venereal disease - which might explain why nowadays, anyone desirous of being admitted into his ashram is requested to undergo a HIV test. This person also has followers in China, and they follow him with the same idea that one can attain spiritual perfection through sex.[52] From the perspective of Patanjali's teachings, these persons are not practicing Yoga. Real love is selfless by nature, whereas sex is just the opposite.[53] We all have seen dogs fighting over a bitch; it is not love that motivates them. The sex drive is a strong force and it is in the mode of

51 http://quotes.gaia.com/osho_bhagwan_shree_rajneesh
52 http://tantraecstasy.blogspot.com/2007/12/tantra-as-therapy-was-osho-wrong.html
53 Sex is meant for reproduction – done for this purpose it can become a spiritual act (Bg 7.11)

passion. It keeps the living being bound to the mistaken identification with the body. The effort to satisfy this desire of the flesh leads to more craving, a symptom generally seen in any type of addiction. An addicted person is willing to do and say anything to get his dose.

Prabhupada explains: "Life in the material world is maintained by sucking one's own blood. The central point of attraction for material enjoyment is sex life. To enjoy sex life is to suck one's own blood, and there is not much more to be explained in this connection. The camel also sucks its own blood while chewing thorny twigs. The thorns the camel eats cut the tongue of the camel, and so blood begins to flow within the camel's mouth. The thorns, mixed with fresh blood, create a taste for the foolish camel, and so he enjoys the thorn-eating business with false pleasure." (SB 2.3.19 p)

U. G. Krishnamurti, a writer and philosopher whose teachings are more recognized outside of India than at home, is another example of fabricated ideas. About the *atma* he says: "I discovered for myself and by myself that there is no self to realize - that's the realization I am talking about. Self-knowledge or self-realization is to realize for yourself and by yourself that there is no self to realize - that is going to be a shattering blow. To realize that there is no enlightenment at all is enlightenment."[54] Such nihilistic explanations certainly go against the traditional teachings that have guided people of India since time immemorial. Can one be benefited by a person who derides the wisdom of his own ancestors?

Information about the *atma* and Isvara are beyond the knowledge we can get through our senses. Material senses have their limitations, and to properly understand subjects beyond their purview we require authoritative sources. Conclusive Truth is revealed in the *Vedas*, first and foremost in the *Vedanta-Sutra* and its natural commentary, known as *Srimad- Bhagavatam*, and in the Bhagavad-gita. Anyone who studies these books can rightly expound the Ultimate Truth. To

54 http://www.mindisamyth.com

perceive the Absolute Truth with His energies and engage everything in His service is the correct understanding of reality and the foundation of Bhakti Yoga. Referring to monists and nihilists, Prabhupada writes: "They refuse to accept that the living entity has an individual existence separate from that of the Supreme. Thus, they have created confusion all over the world, because their conclusion is mundane and against the very nature of the transcendental process of Bhakti Yoga, pure devotional service. (CC Adi 7.114)

The defect of such thinkers is their erroneous idea that when the Absolute expands He loses His completeness. This is a material concept and it is not supported by the *Vedas*. The *Brihad-aranyaka Upanisad* states, *purnam idam purnat purnam udacyate:* "Although He expands in many ways, He keeps His original personality. His original spiritual body remains as it is." Similarly, elsewhere it is stated, *vicitra-saktih purusah puranah*: "The Supreme, the original person (*purusha*), has multifarious energies." Many verses can be quoted from the *Upanisads* and the *Vedas* to show that the Supreme at no stage becomes dissolved or loses His personal aspect. Actually, the personal aspect is stressed. In the *Katha Upanisad* (2.2.13) it is said, *nityo nityanam cetanas cetananam eko bahunam yo vidadhati kaman:* "He is the supreme eternally conscious person, who maintains all other living entities." From these *Vedic* references one can understand that the Absolute Truth has personal features and that no one can equal or excel Him. Although foolish philosophers may think themselves to be even greater than the Isvara, He is *asamaurdhva*: no one is equal to or above Him.

Even though Patanjali's Yoga-Sutras speak of *kaivalya* (isolation), it simply means that one should become detached from matter. One should not misunderstand the meaning and commit the mistake of declaring oneself to be identical with the Absolute. As pointed out, if we were the Absolute, then why would we fall into the illusion of identifying ourselves with the material body? This would mean that material nature is more powerful than Isvara, which would negate His supremacy. That cannot be. According to the Bhagavad-gita, we are separated parts, and simultaneously linked up with the Isvara - *mamaivamso jiva-loke; jiva-bhutah sanatanah* (Bg 15.7). That means we are one with Him in quality but not in quantity - He is the whole and we are parts of the whole.

By not referring to standard teachings, which have been recognized as such since time immemorial, many modern so-called Yoga teachers, create confusion. They themselves are in the grip of mistaken paradigms, usually motivated by, and centered on, personal gain. A true spiritual leader, however, does not take the post of spiritual authority for his or her selfish benefit. He or she accepts it as a service in the mood of devotion, in Bhakti Yoga. But for one who does not recognize the personal aspect of the Absolute, what can the motivation be for taking up such a service? Simply the desire for profit and adoration. A genuine teacher is free from such mundane motives, and he accepts the service of his students not for himself but on behalf of the Supreme Isvara. He does not try to derive personal benefit from the students' service but hands all of it over to the Isvara - even the affection he receives from his students - understanding himself to be a mere representative of the Isvara. On the other hand, if one's understanding of the Isvara is impersonal, the Bhakti Yoga process cannot work and becomes a self-deceptive, external show. A teacher devoid of a service attitude to the Isvara (Krishna) might be speaking of "loving all" and "compassion to all" and even quote the Bhagavad-gita or other Yoga texts, but factually he is leading his followers away from actually loving Krishna. Personal or impersonal paradigm - it makes a big difference.

Yoga at Risikesh

CHAPTER TWELVE

ENCOUNTERING - The Isvara

We already pointed out that the system of Astanga-Yoga is closely allied to Sankhya philosophy. We mentioned that when Patanjali speaks about an Absolute Truth he does not discuss in detail what he means by *Isvara* and *Purusha*.

We cited in this book the six branches of thoughts,[55] which are *Vedic* in the sense that they rest on the authority of the *Vedas*. All of these six philosophies accept the idea of an eternal soul that undergoes multiple incarnations, governed by a law of Karma and the idea that the soul should move towards "liberation". They also accept, to varying degrees, that there is an eternal Cause, an Isvara, responsible for the existence of the phenomenal world. Now, let us try to understand what exactly that *Isvara* is.

For knowing Him we suggest you read the Bhagavad-gita and *Srimad-Bhagavatam*, the quintessence of all the *Vedas*, because they contain detailed information about Him. These writings introduce us to the interactions of the Isvara with His individual parts and parcels in their liberated state. *Srimad-Bhagavatam*, especially, gives detailed records of such pastimes (*lilas*), which are always devoid of any tinge of mundanity. By hearing them one learns to distinguish reality from illusion (*maya*) and one develops attraction for the Isvara (usually referred to as "Krishna" in those texts), thus making progress towards pure love.

In the original texts of Sankhya philosophy, on the other hand, one does not find descriptions of an active Isvara. The term *sankhya* literally means "to count."

55 The Six Philosophies are: 1) Nyaya (logic), 2) Vaiseṣika (atomic theory), 3) Sankhya (analysis of matter and spirit), 4) Yoga (the discipline of self-realization), 5) Karma-mimamsa (the science of fruitive work) and 6) Vedanta (the science of Isvara realization).

It is mainly an analytical study of the material world that allows one to understand the different features of matter, and thereby what eternal spirit is. The earliest available text of Sankhya teachings, the *Sankhya-karika*, does not even mention an Isvara. Some conclude that the early Sankhya philosophers did not accept His existence, but from later texts one understands that they did. Perhaps, the Sankhya philosophers were persuaded in debates, because it is difficult to explain the origin of a universe without including the concept of an Isvara.

However, Patanjali's acceptance of the existence of an Isvara seems to be limited to a particular aspect of that Isvara. Thus, he describes the Isvara as "the perfect Supreme Being who is eternal, all-pervading, omnipotent, omniscient, and omnipresent. That being, unlike us, is not affected by the afflictions of ignorance, egoism, desire, aversion, and fear of death. He is also free from all karmic action, from the results of action, and from all latent impressions." (YS 1.24-26). Still, since there is no *lila* (pastime description) in Patanjali's Sutras we can conclude that he is not aware of the complete feature of the Isvara. Patanjali's realizations seem to be limited to the realization of Brahman and Paramatma. We will now discuss these features. (Fig. 11)

Fig. 11: The Brahman and Paramatma features of the Isvara.

Three mantras of the *Mundaka Upanisad* (2.2.9- 11) explain the Brahman feature of the Isvara: "In the spiritual realm, beyond the material covering, is the unlimited Brahman effulgence, which is free from material contamination. That effulgent white light is understood by transcendentalists to be the light of all lights. In that realm there is no need of sunshine, moonshine, fire or electricity for illumination. Indeed, whatever illumination appears in the material world is only a reflection of that supreme illumination. That Brahman is in front and at the back, in the north, south, east and west, and also overhead and below. In other words, that supreme Brahman effulgence spreads throughout both the material and spiritual skies."

We have already discussed the Paramatma feature of the Isvara: the controlling aspect that deals with the material nature and the law of Karma. The

Brahman aspect is an additional realization, usually included when one realizes the Paramatma aspect. Bhakti Yoga philosophy teaches three aspects of the Isvara that, taken together, make for complete realization of the Isvara: Brahman, Paramatma, and Bhagavan. (SB 1.2.11) To say it in other words: 1) I understand I'm an eternal soul and not this body (*sat*); 2) I'm subordinate to the Paramatma (*cit*); and 3) I'm a spiritual participant in ongoing loving exchanges with the Isvara (*ananda-lila*). Full realization is *sat-cit-ananda* – eternity, cognition, and bliss.

Patanjali, in his Yoga-sutras, gives little indication of a blissful union with that Isvara. He speaks only of the *kaivalya* state of perfection, a state of freedom from matter. (YS 2.25; 3.50; 4.26; 4.30) From the view point of Bhakti Yoga, this attainment is not the highest perfection. *Kaivalya* constitutes the line of demarcation between the world of limitation and the transcendental world. By Bhakti Yoga one goes beyond this and attains the diversity of the spiritual world. The mere removal of the miseries that arise from mundane life does not result in true life and eternal happiness. The real gain for the *atma* is to revert to his original, eternal existence in his realized state, which is loving union with the Isvara. This state is attained by the practice of Bhakti Yoga only, and not by any other Method.

CHAPTER THIRTEEN

EMPLOYING - The Vedic Paradigm

As explained in Chapter Ten, each individual tends to have a particular paradigm or viewpoint, or to be more precise his or her own point of view. We have become conditioned to look at things around us from our particular viewpoint. However, what we see is only a limited aspect of the whole range of space and time. Furthermore, we are only able to see the immediate cause of the events that take place around us, and we are unable to recognize the remote cause. To illustrate this point, take for example a domino stone falling over. The immediate cause of its falling was the stone next to it, which had fallen over. However, from a perspective further away, we are able to see the whole wall of domino stones falling down one by one - how one stone pushes the stone immediately next to it, causing them all to fall. We are now thus able to perceive the remote cause. An even more comprehensive and objective study of the event would lead us to understand that the last stone in the line fell because of the first one being initially pushed by someone's hand.

How we are able to see the immediate cause of an event but generally fail to see the remote cause applies to this world and its creator. To understand the cause of all causes, one would have to go beyond time and space. One would have to be all-cognizant, that is to say, have access to the past, present, and future. This, in fact, is the vision the Isvara and pure-minded persons have. Consequently, in order to obtain true knowledge of what is reality, we have to take note of what is said by Him - or about Him by those who are close to Him.

Parts of the *Vedas*, especially *Srimad-Bhagavatam* and the Bhagavad-gita, give us exactly that kind of insight: By hearing we get to know the Isvara and His perspective. The *Bhagavatam* explains in detail how that Isvara, known as Krishna, with His body made of pure cognizance and unlimited potencies, is able to create unlimited, different forms of Himself, called "expansions." Furthermore, He is able, without diminishing Himself in any way, to expand Himself by creating innumerable entities, each of whom possesses varying portions of His own creative potencies. It is further stated that there are millions of such expansions but that for the sake of understanding them, they are broadly categorized into two: *plenary* expansions and *atma* expansions. The former are essentially the same as Krishna, whereas expansions of the *atma* kind are the individual souls like you and me. There is also a third energy, His "shadow" energy, which is manifested in the form of gross and subtle matter. That matter causes forgetfulness of the reality and covers the *atma*'s original knowledge with illusory ideas, causing one to be in a dream-like state. (SB 2.5.19)

Isvara literally means "master," "controller," and Patanjali refers to Him as that special person or enjoyer (*Purusha*) who is forever free and uncontaminated (YS 1.24). One can get additional information from *Vedic* texts such as, for example, the *Brahma-samhita*: *Isvarah paramah krishnah sat-cid-ananda-vigrahah:* "Krishna, known as Govinda, is the Supreme Controller. He has an eternal, blissful, spiritual body." - *anadir adir govindah sarva-karana-karanam*: "He is the origin of all. He has no other origin and He is the prime cause of all causes." (*Brahma-samhita* 5.1)

A question arises: "Should one take such description literally or is it a symbolic description only? Is Krishna really the cause of all the phenomenal and spiritual worlds? Are we, the *atmas*, linked with Him? In what way are we linked with Him?" Actually, these statements are factual, but we should also understand that in our conditioned state - with our spiritual mind and senses covered by the material modes of nature - we cannot understand the literal meaning of this verse. Yet, even though we only grasp some mundane meaning - a perverted and distorted version of what is really being said - the language remains real and valid. And even though we cannot grasp the language that is used to describe that Isvara, we should use it, for such usage purifies our minds and senses, so that we will eventually come to understand fully what we speak. Unlike the speculators (*jnanis*), the Bhakti Yogi accepts the *Vedic* statements literally, and his intelligence thus gets purified so that eventually he comes to fully understand their meaning.

Those of you who are familiar with Yoga and Indian culture might know about Siva and wonder what his position in the Universe is. Siva is often confused to be the cause of everything. However, that is not the fact. He is not the "*Isvarah paramah*" that we described above. Every one of us is an expansion of the Supreme, including Siva. Everything is an expansion of Krishna's energy. True, Siva is called *Mahesvara*, (*Maha* = great; *Isvara* = controller) because he is the superintendent of the mode of ignorance (*tamo-guna*). He takes charge of destroying the universe at the time scheduled for its annihilation. One should see everything and every living entity, including Brahma and Siva, as simultaneous one and different from the Supreme Truth. In other words, everything in existence is an expansion of Krishna's energy. The above information about Krishna as the ultimate Isvara is spoken by Brahma. To appreciate the actual value of the information Brahma gave us, we will do well to take note of his position in the Universe. We should know how tiny our position is in comparison with Him. He is the first being in the Universe and has a lifespan of 311 trillion years. Contrary to what many people believe, it is not that the world and everything came into being from the primitive stage. We did not evolve from prehistoric apes. For our education, let us at this point, look into how the *Vedas* explain the process of creation.

A Sadhu

CHAPTER FOURTEEN

BEGINNING - The Journey

Brahma is the original conscious being in the universe, an *atma* that holds the topmost executive post in the universe. His body is made primarily of the subtle material elements, unlike our bodies, which are made of gross matter. He has the task of creating bodies for the other conscious selves existing at various levels of the cosmic hierarchy. From the body of Brahma come great sages, sometimes known as his mental sons. Brahma creates a female and the granddaughters born from his daughter become the wives of some of the sages. They produce generations of demigods and demigoddesses, with bodies composed primarily of the subtle material energy. These demigods and demigoddesses, by their reproductive processes, produce the forms of living things, including humans, who reside on our earth planet. In their reproductive processes, they make use of *bijas*, or mental seeds, which contain essential elements (seen by some as RNA and DNA) for building the various bodies.

In recent years, some scientists came up with the "Intelligent Design Version" of creation, a concept that opposes Darwinian thinking.[56] They want to prove that before matter arranged itself into proteins and microbes, intelligence already existed. The idea of "Intelligence before Matter" is part of the *Vedic* version. The Isvara (*paramatma*-aspect), assisted by demigods, governs the ongoing process of creation, maintenance, and dissolution of the universe.

People tend to accept various explanations for the origin of human life. They either accept the simple evolutionary account (we are evolved chemicals that somehow evolved into apes, who in turn evolved into humans), a simplistic creation account (God created everything instantly *ex nihilo*), or the

56 Michel Behe, Darwin's Black Box: *The Biochemical Challenge to Evolution*
Http://www.arn.org/authors/behe.html

extraordinarily imaginative ET account. The actual story may be more complex, as we see in the devolution account, which involves all three things, i.e., some overall control by a Supreme Cosmic Intelligence, a process of evolution (i.e. reproduction with modification, but going from top down rather than bottom up, and involving mind and consciousness in addition to matter), and finally an extraterrestrial or extra-dimensional aspect to the whole process, with all three things woven together in a interesting pattern.[57]

The *Vedic* explanation of creation is astounding and most scientific. In fact, the *Vedas* describe many amazing things. There are incidents of remarkable nature that took place on this earth, some time in the remote past. Many of these events involve phenomena that ordinary persons do not experience today. One might ask why this is so, if these events actually did occur at one time. One reason given in *Srimad-Bhagavatam* is that prior to the present age people had higher sensory powers and had connections with higher beings. The age we are in now began around 5000 years ago and is known as the "Iron Age" (*Kali Yuga*). It is an age of materialism without much spiritual culture. Because of the decline of spiritual awareness the linkage with higher beings has almost entirely disappeared.

The scenario then is that, for a while, people remembered the earlier state of affairs on the earth in the form of narrations but gradually these were also forgotten. Now in the present stage of civilization old traditions are widely viewed as useless mythology. People now accept anything as fact only via information received through their gross senses or through beliefs that have no factual foundations. Even worse, many people assume that there was never a time in the past when humans were as advanced as we are at present, what to speak of more advanced. Little do they know that just the opposite is true! Humanity is presently in the most degraded stage. Humans are becoming more and more selfish and violent - to animals (animal farms) and to other humans (genocides).

What makes modern man think that the world has come into being as a unique event that has somehow occurred by chance? On what basis do we assume that life is to be found only on this planet? Another coincidence? Why should one believe such proposals? Yogic philosophy teaches us that the creation of universes and planets is not a linear one-time event but a cyclic process. As we have continuous cycles of seasons year after year, so the process of creation is a continuous, ongoing event. There are many creations and

57 Adapted from http://humandevolution.com

subcreations that take place again and again. Thus, even before our present manifested creation, all these bodily forms of different species already existed.

Beyond this world of matter is the cause of all causes - the Isvara. He is the eternal principle, and because He has spiritual senses with which He interacts in spiritual surroundings - the spiritual, eternal world to which we all originally belong - He can respond to our love. Yoga teaches one how to reach that spiritual abode. A pilgrimage to holy places in India is a good start, because many holy places there, although apparently situated within the phenomenal world, are in fact purely spiritual. Thus, in spite of our limited awareness of the sublime position of such places, their spiritually surcharged atmosphere purifies our consciousness, thus paving the way for our final journey - the journey to that eternal and blissful spiritual world.

Walking Barefoot

CHAPTER FIFTEEN

Ending - The Journey

In the Astanga-Yoga system one has to vigorously practice and, at the appropriate time, leave the body to travel through space to ever higher planets, finally reaching *Siddhaloka* (*Satyaloka*) (Bg 8.24-27). The Yoga view of the universe (cosmology) is very precise and detailed. From that view we understand that, alongside our tiny earth planet, there are countless bigger planets, and the Yogi bypasses all of them to reach the topmost planet of the universe, where Lord Brahma resides. Details of the journey are given in *Srimad-Bhagavatam* (2.2.24). It states there that the Yogis become cleansed of all dirty things acquired in the phenomenal world through contact with the fire demigod. That demigod marks the path of liberation, which is called *arciradi-vartma* (SB 8.5.36).

Arciradi refers to the path of light in which the first deity is *Arci*, the deva of light. Altogether there are thirteen more deities on the path of light. The Yogi moves along the path from one deity to the next, never to return. These deities give passage-permission to that Yogi and he offers appropriate worship. The Milky Way seen in the sky is the path leading to the highest planet of the universe. The phenomenal world is described as dark, but beyond the phenomenal world is a bright existence. In other words, after passing through the dark material

atmosphere, one comes to the luminous spiritual sky. That effulgence is known as *Siddhaloka*. Yogis such as Patanjali, by strictly following the Astanga-Yoga system, can reach that *Siddhaloka*. When Lord Brahma, who resides in that place, reaches the end of his life he goes together with these Yogis to the spiritual world, which is full of variety.

We should mention at this point that the process for spiritual elevation is twofold: it is enacted internally and simultaneously also on a cosmic scale. We are situated within a multidimensional cosmos, and we are not limited to the linear dimension. The Isvara is within and without (*antar bahir avasthitam*). The Vedic literature maintains that we live in a hierarchically structured universe occupied by 400,000 species of human-like forms, and some 8,000,000 nonhuman species. These living beings inhabit a graded system of worlds, which possess variegated geographical features. The thesis of the *Vedas* is that these worlds are literally real, even though they are almost entirely inaccessible to ordinary human senses.

Still there is a corresponding principle involving microcosm (the body) and macrocosm (the universe and the universal form). Prabhupada writes in *Srimad-Bhagavatam* that "Yogis worship the Sisumara planetary system, which is technically known as the Kundalini-cakra." (SB 5.23 summary). It means that Yogis in meditation identify the central axis of the universe with the series of cakras in the spinal column. By moving their life airs up the series of cakras, they prepare their subtle bodies to travel up the axis of the universe to *Satyaloka*, (*Siddhaloka*).[58]

Other *Vedic* texts confirm this understanding: "There are one hundred and one subtle pranic channels emanating from the heart. One of these - the susumna - extends to the top of the head. By passing up through this channel, one transcends death. The other channels lead in all directions to various kinds of rebirth." (Chandogya Upanisad 8.6.6).

As explained above, the Yogi then leaves his gross body through the 101st coronary artery and he moves along the path of light from one planet to the next. Patanjali explains in the third chapter how, by practice of Astanga Yoga, one can access higher realms and attain mystical powers. Because the body is a miniature presentation of the cosmos, whatever exists in the cosmos is also present in the body. Microcosm and macrocosm being one, an individual can thus have access to the powers of the universe. The Bhakti-Yogi, however, is different in that he does not desire such powers but only wants loving reciprocation with the highest Isvara. Because that Isvara is always beyond the phenomenal world, the Bhakti-Yogi can, by the strength of his absorption, transcend temporary existence. He is not much impressed by mystical feats, which tend to bind one to the phenomenal world.

Many unscrupulous persons attract and cheat people by a display of mystic powers. The typical pattern (at least in India) is that a person begins to exhibit genuine mystic powers. When praised by naive followers, he develops an inflated ego and presents himself as a divine incarnation. In many instances, the person later loses his powers, and he then resorts to cheap tricks to live up to his follower's expectations. This, of course, goes in favor of skeptics, who put forward such cases to demonstrate the futility of spiritual practices.

58 *Kundalini* and *Cakras*: Modern Yoga societies proudly advertise "Raise your *Kundalini*," as if this would be so simple. In reality, one can get seriously injured by prematurely evoking these energy circles.

CHAPTER SIXTEEN

UPGRADING - What Others Do Not Teach

In Chapter Nine we discussed freedom of choice and how we make use of it - we desire and make efforts. In Chapter Eleven we heard of teachings proclaiming that nothing exists, not even an eternal soul. Actually, it is possible to reach such a state of awareness. It is called "*Sunya*," and it is a phase in the process of creation, prior to matter taking shape and variety. It is not a spiritual platform at all; it is simply a stage of undeveloped matter: "In the unmanifest stage of material nature, called *pradhana*, there is no expression of words, no mind, and no manifestation of the subtle elements beginning from the *mahat*, nor the modes of goodness, passion, and ignorance. There is no life air or intelligence, nor any senses or demigods. There is no definite arrangement of planetary systems, and the different stages of consciousness - sleep, wakefulness and deep sleep - are absent. There is no ether, air, fire, water, earth, nor sun. The situation is just like that of complete sleep, or of voidness. Indeed, it is indescribable. Authorities in spiritual science explain, however, that since *pradhana* is the original substance, it is the actual basis of material creation." (SB 12.4.20-21).

To come to the awareness of a primordial substance is not spiritual. Despite the fact that one basically becomes non-existent by this achievement, since one takes on the qualities of dead matter, for some persons this idea is an appealing proposal that would solve the problem of differences in this world: if everything in life were realized as unreal there would be fewer conflicts. If ultimately every variety of form and names were to be understood as an illusion, then one indeed could embrace any form of practice and conviction, because essentially one would never truly accept anything, save and except the idea that "all that exists is an illusion."

This proposal, although alluring, requires one to give up all conceivable attributes, feelings, and finally give up thought itself. Although an absurd proposition, the idea of an ultimate void and the intent to destroy feelings is widely accepted as very spiritual. Aware of the difficulty in practicing anything with this type of understanding, many spiritual teachers keep up the concept of specific forms of gods and goddesses, even if they are to serve as symbols only. They think it is helpful for progress on the path, so let us keep it. According to them, images, deities, and prayers are useful symbolic expressions with no real meaning. What is recorded and narrated as historic events, the description of the cosmos and the journey to higher planets, all should be seen as mythological and symbolic.

Because such modern spiritual teachers are desirous to attract followers but at the same time realize the difficulty of strictly practicing anything, they therefore include the elements of Bhakti Yoga into their teachings. For example, they do *kirtan* (chanting) or hear about the *lilas* (pastimes) of the Isvara. However, it should be known that they are faking Bhakti; they do not accept an ultimate reality consisting of a personal Absolute. They are so deeply convinced of their paradigm that they can hardly consider the possibility of a reality with variety beyond undifferentiated matter.

I remember being in the presence of a teacher with just that conviction. Several of us took a tour of a Krishna temple in India, and we had this teacher as our guide. As we walked around, we observed a group of devout Indians offering prayers and songs to the deities in the temple. Our guide, a bit embarrassed by their sincerity and devotion, worriedly tried to explain to us that these simple people have little education in spiritual matters. He implied that if they had been more educated they would not be engaged in such emotional activities. He assumed we would agree with him but we did not. We made it clear to him that he should upgrade himself to the level of proper understanding of what Bhakti Yoga is.

The paradigm this person had in his mind was that of an Isvara without any personal features, a result which is achieved by the process of abstraction and negation. By mental considerations and speculations, this person's normal and natural spiritual feelings had become crippled and limited. He was unable to understand that the simple people whom we observed were carrying within their hearts spontaneous faith and sincerity. Whereas Bhakti impels one to relate to the Isvara with feeling and a sense of kinship, speculation leads one to become silent and dry. Since the negative abstraction about the nature of the Absolute presupposes that language originates here, in our traffic with the objects of this world, it is assumed that language has no competence to deal with something beyond matter. They think that when one uses language to speak of the spiritual, it snaps as an overstretched rubber band does.

Such ideas are widespread, but from the point of view of Bhakti they are wrong. Bhakti understands that the language conveying the names, forms, attributes, and activities of the transcendent Isvara does not originate in this world. The origin of everything is He, and the original use of language is to praise, glorify, and offer prayers to Him.[59] Service to Him is the proper and original use of everything. Forgetting that service to the Isvara, one perverts the language by using it for sense objects in this world only. Please refer to our discussion in Chapter Thirteen on whether one should take words that describe the Isvara literally or symbolically.

When the Isvara becomes known, and inspires one to speak about Him and to Him, language is restored to its original use. It is transcendental speech, and it must be practiced with seriousness. Real teachers of Bhakti Yoga say that our materially contaminated mind and senses cannot comprehend the transcendental quality of the names, attributes, and so on, of the Isvara, but that when our senses -- beginning with the tongue - have become purified by being engaged in the practice of Bhakti Yoga, by the grace of the Supreme Isvara, one becomes aware of the spiritual qualities of His names and attributes. The *Srimad-Bhagavatam* confirms this: "The speculators, the *jnanis*, go on speculating about the Supreme for many, many hundreds of thousands of years, but unless one is favored by the Supreme, one cannot understand His supreme glories." (SB 10.14.29). In other words, only the proper execution of Bhakti brings one to the level of actual contact with the personal feature of the Absolute.

Another unfortunate misunderstanding, because of negative abstraction, is the notion that one cannot render service to the Absolute because He has no senses. How to relate to something or someone unable to perceive anything? They rightly conclude it is not possible. Therefore, persons who believe that the Absolute has no senses advocate instead selfless service to man (*Manavah*), not to the Isvara (*Madhava*). "*Manavah seva* equals *Madhava seva*" is their well-known

---

59 Appendix Three shows a practical application of this understanding

slogan. But we must be aware that this concept is not in accord with the principles of Bhakti Yoga. No doubt, selfless actions have a purifying effect and elevate one to the mode of goodness. It also gives good karmic reactions; however, to be spiritual there must be a tangible link (Yoga) with the Isvara. Only in such a situation will our actions become spiritual. Patanjali says that one has to carefully consider the meaning of Isvara and chant His Holy Name. Similarly, the Bhagavad-gita says one has to think of Krishna (9.26, 18.65) while acting in this world. Bhakti Yoga is more than doing good works in this world; it is the work done for the Isvara (also named Madhava), and in order to do so we need to be aware of Him.

To help us understand how a purified Bhakti-Yogi perceives this world and its relationship with the Isvara, we can use as an example an experience most of us have likely had. Say we watch a movie in a cinema and get absorbed in the happenings on the screen, namely the visuals and sounds. The absorbing experience is possible because we have become unaware of everything except the screen, a situation created by the darkness that surrounds us. In that condition we are not aware that the lights we see are coming from behind us, from a point where someone is operating the movie projector. All we see is the screen. Likewise, when our minds are in the lower modes (ignorance and passion), we do not realize that in the background of this world is the Isvara. Fascinated by the daily happenings in our lives, we have little realization of anything else. We do not realize that what exists in reality is only the Isvara with His energies. All we see at present are things that seem to be separated from Him.

The Bhakti-Yogis understand the accuracy of the cinema example. Bhakti-Yogis do not say that the movie of the world is an illusion. Again, the example of the cinema helps us understand the situation: What happens when the darkness in the cinema hall gives way to bright lights? The lights from the projector are still there, we individuals are still seated in our chairs, but now we realize that what is occurring on the screen in front of us is illusory. Now that the darkness has gone, the movie has lost its fascination. Thus, reality means to see the Isvara and His energies at work. It is wrong to think that everything is unreal, or that we are the enjoyers of the things in this world; if we think so we beckon this illusion towards us. Our meditation should be on how to use the material body and the objects in this world in the service of the Isvara. That mood is Bhakti Yoga. It will lead to awareness of the Isvara, and this awareness will instantly free us from all the binding forces of this temporary world of darkness.

Prabhupada writes: "The vision of the devotees is not ordinary; it is purified by the process of devotional service. In other words, as the universal elements are both within and without, similarly the Lord's name, form, quality, pastimes, entourage, etc., as they are described in the revealed scriptures or as performed in the *Vaikuṇṭha-lokas* (spiritual planets), far, far beyond the material cosmic manifestation, are factually being televised in the heart of the devotee. The man with a poor fund of knowledge cannot understand, although by material science one can see things far away by means of television. Factually, the spiritually developed person is able to have the television of the kingdom of God always reflected within his heart. That is the mystery of knowledge of the Personality of Godhead." (SB 2.9.35 p)

CHAPTER SEVENTEEN

REVIEWING - The Foolproof Path

Let us review and summarize some of the ideas discussed in the last chapters. We have pointed out that there are specific ways by which the Yogi leaves the world and enters the higher planets. We pointed out that there are no unreal features about the process of spiritual life, the cosmos, and the Absolute Truth. We gave some insight and warnings about the misleading ideas of many modern Yoga teachers who teach that there is no reality beyond matter and that matter has to be dismantled to achieve perfection, which according to them is the state of oneness or non-existence. We came to understand how the true Bhakti Yoga teachers seek to correct these misunderstandings and how they try to foster the development of pure Bhakti Yoga without speculative ideas.

We have addressed the mistaken fear many people have that such fostering of Bhakti injures the unified spirit of all races and cultures. Bhakti, with its conceptually specific object of devotion, is not, as wrongly assumed, responsible for sectarian exclusivity and hostility. We objected to the misconceived alternative of focusing on an Absolute Oneness and to the wrong notion that the world we experience is unreal. We hinted at the idea that we need not accept indiscriminately all forms of spiritual life as equally valid.

We showed how Bhakti does not devalue individuality, diversity, and relativity as such. We made the point that such characteristics are found in this world because they exist in the origin. Bhakti, Isvara, the individual souls, and the relations between Him and them are all eternal, irreducible, and ultimately real. We should know how He sustains ongoing, ever-developing loving relationships and how He discloses Himself in different ways, according to the nature of the relationship. "As they surrender to Me, I reward them accordingly." (Bg. 4.11) We showed how we do not need to propagate ideas of emptiness to be liberal, broad-minded, and tolerant. If the sectarian intolerance of some devotional communities is actually a consequence of their Bhakti, then it is owing to too little, rather than too much of it. In other words, because such practitioners are not very advanced, they sometimes come across as intolerant. The fault is not their Bhakti; it is their lack of it.

In conclusion, the factual Bhakti-Yogi is the most liberal because, as a practitioner, he recognizes the differences between people as being due to the difference of development in the attainment of purity and perfection. Different attainments are due to the different reciprocation of the Isvara with the individual, which depends on the different kinds of desire and attempt of each person. The advanced Bhakti-Yogi can clearly perceive this through his elevated consciousness. He sees how the law of Karma acts and how the different modes of nature bind us.

Furthermore, we can repeat the point that there is no need to replace devotion with speculation, nor the sentient with an impersonal Absolute, something that many so-called Yoga teachers try to do to make the world a better place. Such ideas are the direct result of the materialistic paradigms rooted in their minds as a consequence of impure desires, which bind them and their followers to the modes of material nature.

We briefly explained how the successful Astanga-Yogi departs from this world by using the mystic power he has attained through the process of Astanga-Yoga. According to Patanjali, one can achieve whatever one wants through the practice of *samyama*, because it expands human potentials and allows one to explore higher and higher states of consciousness (YS 3.4). The Vedic literature contains many references to the idea of traveling from planet to planet through outer space. For some Yogis it is possible to travel from one part of the universe to another by the direct use of mystic *siddhis*. No machines are required, and the empowered being is able to transcend the constraints of ordinary space and time.

The *Bhagavatam*, however, explains that on his path of ascent the progressive living entity enters the different planets and has to take birth on each one (*bhutva bhutva* - having repeated birth). As mentioned in Chapter Fifteen, he also has to offer appropriate worship to the deities in these planets. Finally, after he enters *Brahmaloka*, he enjoys life for many millions of years, and then his material designation ends. He comes to a subtle designation, from which he attains the causal designation, witnessing all previous states. Upon the annihilation of this causal state, he attains his pure state, in which he identifies with the Isvara. In this way the living entity becomes transcendental (SB 7.15.54-55).

In contrast to all these Yogis, those in the mood of Bhakti Yoga get direct passage to the spiritual world, without any separate endeavors nor worship of any devas. The *Vedas*, especially the *Bhagavatam*, relate many incidents supporting this version. One such example is Dhruva Maharaja who, even as a small boy, achieved this perfection. Another example is Ajamila who, by performing only a fraction of Bhakti, received guidance that enabled him to further practice Bhakti and to achieve perfection at the end of life.

Prabhupada comments in this regard that Bhakti Yoga is so potent that by adopting these principles of life one can very easily go back to the spiritual world. He says that by Bhakti Yoga one makes an "easy journey to other planets" and ultimately goes back to Godhead. "Devotees have no interest in seeing other planets, but while going back to Godhead they see all of them as passing phases, just as one who is going to a distant place passes through many small stations." (SB 4.12.25) How could it be so easy? Because one gets help from the highest abode; one gets mercy. (see Chapter Five on the Yoga Ladder)

At this stage, I would like to share an important point with you, dear reader, which you might put to good use in your own practice of Bhakti Yoga. Over my two decades of practice of Bhakti Yoga I have come to recognize that among different practitioners in different parts of the world are a number of individuals who always declare that they have a "unique" advantage over others due to the mercy of an especially elevated "Savior-Guru." This phenomenon occurs amongst Bhakti Yoga practitioners and others.[60]

According to them, it is by the strength of the purity of the Guru that one makes advancement - and their Guru, of course, is the topmost. They assume that it is their master who burns up their past Karma, but factually it is not exactly like that. Only the Supreme Isvara is able to neutralize the reaction of past sinful deeds, whether one's own or those of one's dependents - children or disciples. The Isvara neutralizes the reaction for someone engaged in serious Bhakti Yoga, which means that ultimately we should rise to this very platform. (SB 8.24.53p)

The "Savior-Guru" idea has to be considered carefully. There is no doubt in my mind about the saving grace of the spiritual master. After undergoing countless births in different forms of life, when we finally meet and learn from such a teacher, we come to know what the real purpose of life is. Prabhupada says: "To attain perfection in transcendental knowledge is to accept the disciple succession, the spiritual line, by culture, practice, and education in that line." (Message of Godhead, Chapter One)

---

60 http://godsdirectcontact.com/qa/t2.htm - Followers of Ching Hai, a laudable woman engaged in philanthropic work to make the world a better place, call her "Supreme Master." They think: "*We are very safe and have no leakage to let the karma sprout.*" The evidence for this would be that her follower would become free from selfish interest. Does her method actually lead one to this perfection?

Yes, we need to take guidance from a teacher who is expert in the Bhakti Yoga process. Such a teacher will not ask the disciple to go outside the parameters of the Bhakti Yoga process, which is clearly defined by a long tradition. Certain principles should be followed: "One should rise early in the morning, take bath, dress in clean clothes, and meditate on the sound of mantras, such as Hare Krishna, Hare Krishna, Krishna Krishna, Hare Hare; Hare Rama, Hare Rama, Rama Rama, Hare Hare. There are various rules and regulations which one should follow." These *yamas* and *niyamas* are equally important for all Yoga systems. "Additionally, one should regularly hear Bhagavad-gita and *Srimad-Bhagavatam* from persons who are fully conversant with the Bhakti Yoga science. This practice can help anyone rise to the level of pure Bhakti, and then one is sure of his progress into the spiritual realm." (Bg 12.9)

Yet, to think that the acceptance of a teacher alone will save one from past karmic reactions is a misunderstanding. This mistaken idea is shared by the majority of persons who follow some mundane religion and thereby think that they are saved because they have the "right" religion. Rest assured that if they neglect to carefully practice to attract the mercy of the Isvara, they will make no, or only very little, progress. In particular, the practice of proper chanting requires much effort, willpower, and insight, because chanting is really a scientific process. We should be aware of the different stages of chanting: offensive, clearing, and pure. It is the clearing stage of chanting that elevates one to the position of pure chanting. How is this?

The spiritual master opens our eyes with the torchlight of knowledge *(om ajnana timirandhasya)*, and by his guidance we learn to see things as they are. By his grace and our introspection, we become conscious of our faults and learn how to improve. Chanting while trying to give up impure desires is the recommended process for the fallen souls in this age, and the process is known as "Sadhana Bhakti," *Bhakti* in the clearing stage. By this process, combined with the saving grace of both the teacher and the Isvara (Krishna), and sustained by our sincere endeavor, we can successfully overcome all shortcomings. The outcome is that we get the purity and taste to constantly chant and are blessed with the capacity to serve Krishna unconditionally. Then we can be fully confident of receiving whatever help we may still need to successfully complete our journey to the spiritual world. We will get Krishna's mercy.

At present, in our fallen and impure condition, we resemble persons afflicted with jaundice. A jaundiced patient cannot taste the sweetness of sugar - it tastes bitter. When the patient is cured, then again he likes the taste. Similarly, although Bhakti is very satisfying, we might initially not always feel inclined to practice. To compensate for the lack of liking we are advised to invest effort and willpower. Gradually we will recuperate and then be able to experience the sweetness of devotional activities; essentially, we get a taste for chanting the *Maha-Mantra*. Impure and foolish as we now might be, we should not remain so. A student of Prabhupada recalls in his book "My Glorious Master" how, on one occasion, Prabhupada spoke about the humility of advanced Bhakti-Yogis. At that time, the student said: "My only qualification is that I am a fool." Prabhupada then looked at him sharply and replied: "Yes, but you should not remain a fool." (MGM 16).

What is the difficulty? The fact remains, "I am a spirit soul," and therefore all I need to do is act in that capacity. My undying identity is that "I am an eternal associate of the Isvara. My proper occupation is to act for his pleasure. I belong to the transcendental world." *Jivera svarupa haya-kṛṣṇera nitya-dasa* (Cc. Madhya 20.108). With this conviction, one reverts to the healthy condition and ends all foolishness.[61]

61 To deepen your conviction, please contemplate the illustration next to the Yoga Ladder Appendix.

CHAPTER EIGHTEEN

SHARING - The Matchless Treasure

Throughout this book, Yoga is portrayed as a scientific process - a way of life that enables us to purify the mind (*citta*) and to revive our connection (*Yoga*) with the Isvara (*Krishna*). This has been clearly illustrated by referring to ancient books (the *Vedas*) and the teachings and philosophies of accomplished Yoga masters.

However, due to the age of Kali, generally depicted as an age of confusion and quarrel, semblances of Yoga teachings are passed around, commonly labeled as religion. In reality, this is not equal to Yoga. It should be emphasized that Yoga has nothing to do with what common people do or say in the name of religion and "God."

In the following paragraphs, I clarify how the understanding of Yoga and its particular concept of the *Isvara* is entirely different or even opposed to ordinary religions and practices. As has been pointed out on several occasions in the text, our conceptions of things should be correct, deep, and thorough, because conception precedes perception. You might have heard the popular saying "beauty lies in the eye of the beholder." This means that what we perceive are not facts; rather we perceive what we assume it to be. Ordinarily, any type of conception (paradigm) arises from our association with the material energy (*gunas*), and is flawed unless and until we attain purified consciousness. One way in which we can attain flawless consciousness is by hearing from a person with purified consciousness. One thus rises to the reality of spiritual happiness.

You may be thinking, however, that if there was any value in hearing from purified persons, it would have been accepted by academics and leaders and embedded in educational policy. William H. Deadwyler, Ph.D., succinctly points out the universal reason for mistaken ideas: "The problem is that a person's knowledge is relative to his situation. When a person is habituated to sensual enjoyment and to sex, his instruments of perception malfunction, and so he is unable to comprehend or experience his own eternal nature, no matter how outstanding he may otherwise be. Such people are sunk in ignorance so profound, so fundamental, that even their greatest knowledge is really a kind of advancement in ignorance. In spite of repeated failures, they perpetually put forward hopeless and quixotic schemes to bring happiness, and they seem to have an animal-like obliviousness to the essential character of the world. Even though they mislead others, however, they are ultimately not worthy of anger or scorn: they suffer like everyone else."[62]

Reading "Bhakti Yoga Pilgrimage" alongside practicing Yoga is likely to alter previous conception and give rise to fresh views. As you interact with relatives and friends, you might experience their reservation towards your acquired new realizations. Generally intelligent people do not believe in what goes around in the name of religions, so they might scorn you, assuming you have taken to some belief system. How do you then share what you learned? In the following section I tentatively provide some clues as to how to proceed.

For instance, if someone tells me that he does not believe in "God", I ask the person to describe the "God" he does not believe in. In most cases, the description will exactly match the picture of what this Chapter is about: Yoga is dissimilar to common religious beliefs in every aspect. Therefore, I, as a Yoga practitioner, can frankly agree with a disbeliever of religious dogmas regrettably so widespread.

Before describing the concept of "God" that a Yoga practitioner rejects, let us reiterate the Yoga understanding through the use of the analogy of a mountain first looked at from a distance and then close up. The rough shape of the mountain gradually reveals trees and stones to the approaching viewer, and then birds and beasts and other living creatures. In the same way, Brahman, Paramatma, and the Isvara are different feature of the same Truth, differently perceived at different levels of advancement. Bhakti Yoga is the peak of advancement and is manifested

62 Quote from *Endless Love*, BBT; see Acknowledgements

in selfless service to the Isvara with a clear understanding that nothing else exists besides Him and that we, the living entities, are His eternal parts and parcels. Although nothing else exists except the Isvara, He at the same time retains His own individuality and exists eternally distinct from everything. That is the ultimate Mystery and the meaning of "God is Great."

The living being's problem is that he is covered by the illusory energy of the Isvara and thereby unaware of his constitutional position and factual identity, consequently rotating from one temporary body to another until he develops the desire to re-link with the Isvara in Bhakti. To be successful in this attempt, one requires the merciful help of the Isvara by which one can conquer deep-rooted selfishness and the "false ego" (*ahankara*).

Yoga teachings are rational, not dogmatic. Commonly, people are stuck on a certain level of consciousness and do not progress (climb the Ladder), due to lack of qualified leadership. Personal motivation spoils spiritual progress and makes a leader cling to large numbers of followers; the quantity of followers is erroneously taken as an indicator of the person's advancement. However, even Stalin had followers. In the scenario of an unqualified leader, the followers are indoctrinated not to leave the leader lest they lose the "saving grace" and "burn forever." That is not to say one is in a better position by living like an animal with no spiritual goal! Human life is meant for making spiritual progress, to become free from suffering, and to that end, sharing the Yoga treasure is critical. People need to be initiated into the practice of Bhakti Yoga, with initiation marking the beginning of a new lifestyle. Intelligent inquiries form the basis to progress, enabling a person to gradually leave ignorance behind and attain pure consciousness: *prema.* But in Yoga, dogmas have no values. The students stick with the teacher because of his rightful qualification acquired through the training he received from his own Bhakti Yoga teacher.

We will now contrast these teachings with the conceptions that so-called religious people hold in this age of Kali. We are not doing this with the intention to condemn such persons but for our and their education. To begin with, we can safely state that most people do not have an analytical (*Sankhya*) understanding of the difference between matter and spirit (the body and the *atma*), which means that they think that the body or mind is their factual identity. Because of this ignorance they are in constant fear, ultimately of death. They conceive of someone more powerful than they, a "God" that will side with them and save them from enemies, dangers, and reward them with "salvation."[63] Furthermore, most often misery is decoded as a punishment for not being a loyal follower of their chosen "Savior-God" and His law. These days, with the ever-increasing difficulties to meet the daily necessities of life and with little peace of mind, many see signs that time is up and "God" will soon appear to judge all, especially the evil mongers.[64] Little do such persons know about the law of Karma, which, irrespective of any wishful belief, acts upon anyone, incessantly.

An interesting but also distressing characteristic of people with the above conceptions is that they have been around for very long and created havoc in the lives of countless other persons. Anyone conversant with Semitic[65] thoughts and history will be able to confirm that in the name of religion, an incredible amount of violence and cruelty has been, and continues to be, committed. Instead of inspiring a person to become thoughtful and inquisitive about his proper identity, people are converted into some "religion." Countless regions are being conquered under the pretext of religion. Religious zealots project a "God" upon humanity that does not tolerate the worship of any other "God," a "God" who is envious and revengeful.[66]

Could anyone develop loving sentiments for someone depicted in the above manner? Difficult, indeed! The Isvara known to a Yoga student as depicted in the Bhagavad-gita is broadminded and generous. "I am seated in everyone's heart as the Supersoul. As soon as one desires to worship some demigod, I make his faith steady so that he can devote himself to that particular deity." (Bg 7.21) If we look at the Semitic concept of the Isvara in the light of the *Vedic* experience, it is striking how he resembles an *asura*, someone eager to possess and dominate the world (*īśvaro 'ham ahaṁ bhogī,* I am the lord of everything. I am the enjoyer).[67] Instead of wanting to be liberated from false ego, persons who are after power and dominion themselves think they can achieve this by siding with someone who is their powerful leader. Not supporting him or not believing in him is then a crime, and killing such deviators is divine justice. Perhaps a question can be asked at this point: Where has love gone?

---

63 Webster: "Salvation" - the deliverance from the penalty of sin. A person might admit that he is acting improperly but insists that his "Savior-God", not his own effort, can deliver him. This is only partially true, because unless we make sincere efforts, we are not eligible for any help.

64 The day of the last judgment, the end of the world, also known as "doomsday."

65 Judaism, Christianity, and Islam

66 Bible, Exodus 32.27

67 An *asura* is a demonic person. See Bhagavad-Gita, 16.5-19 for a detail description of his character.

Some may object to this gloomy description of the Semitic concept and point out that we do find seekers who reject dogmas and insist on self-knowledge and inner discovery. That is certainly true, but many of them had to pay for their "heresy" by being ruthlessly suppressed by the inquisition. Hence our disclaimer: Yoga teachings have no historical record of selfish motivated violence and are therefore distinct from mundane religions.

It is the search and love for Truth that conquers ignorance. Therefore, the Bhagavad-gita subscribes neither to brute force nor to pacifism but to the active and selfless defense of progressive spiritual life. For this reason alone is Arjuna taking up his weapons to fight - he has no personal interest. Influential persons should be without selfish motive and protect others from sliding down to the modes of ignorance and passion, either by taking weapons against external aggressors, as in the case of Arjuna, and by inspirational teachings to induce people to follow higher values of life, as done by Patanjali Muni and others. In this way, the Bhagavad-gita directs the student to conquer ignorance and concludes with a clear choice: acting in Bhakti Yoga or remaining in illusion. (Bg 18.72-73) Thoughtful persons fail to understand on what grounds people should be deprived from inheriting this treasure of spiritual knowledge once known to humanity and why they should be kept in ignorance, only to become the victims of religious fanatics or disappointed skeptics.

EPILOGUE - Happiness with Bhakti Yoga

A recent study conducted by professors of the British School of Economics proved conclusively that money could buy everything but happiness. The study revealed that people in Bangladesh, one of the poorest countries in the world, derive far more happiness from their small income than, for example, the British do from their relatively large bank balances. In fact, according to the survey, people in more affluent countries such as Austria, Switzerland, Canada, and others are much more unhappy than their poor counterparts in Armenia, Ghana, and other such countries. A small increase in income can mean large improvements in the lifestyle of a poor person and give him some small degree of happiness, but beyond a certain level of income there is no relation between money and happiness. According to the research, happiness in richer countries is dependent on good health, job satisfaction, and close personal relationships.[68] The practice of Yoga fulfills these three needs. I am hopeful that the information contained in this book will be meaningful to the people of China, especially since many people in China have now come to enjoy prosperity.

After reading this book with even a small level of broadmindedness, you will most likely understand that Yoga is not only a part-time practice but also a way of life. Engaging in Yoga exercises in order to maintain good health is fine, but besides that, Bhakti Yoga teaches us how to live and work in a way that links us with the spiritual dimension, thereby giving us a tremendous amount of satisfaction. Being thus situated, we come closer to every living entity, realizing each one to be a part of the Supreme Truth. Thus, we end up feeling close to all living entities. The actual result of practicing Bhakti Yoga is peace and happiness. Prabhupada explains - in the preface to his "Nectar of Devotion", a treatise on Bhakti Yoga: "The Nectar of Devotion" teaches us the science of loving every one of the living entities perfectly by the easy method of loving Krishna. We have failed to create peace and harmony in human society, even by such great attempts

68 The Word Happiness Survey, published in the Indian newspaper Deccan Herald

as the United Nations, because we do not know the right method. The method is very simple, but one has to understand it with a cool head."

The culture of Bhakti Yoga has been seriously neglected in India, chiefly due to the influence of the age of Kali. Any pilgrim to India is exposed to what is now known as "the religion of the Hindus." He or she might be fascinated by the variety of practices and worship abounding everywhere, but the majority of people, in India and elsewhere too, possess little insight into what they are supposed to do with their lives. They blindly practice some kind of religion without philosophical understanding. They might know that there is a Brahma, a Shiva, and a Vishnu (Krishna) but have only vague ideas of what their positions are. Neither do they consider that we are originally pure units of consciousness existing in harmonious connection with the Supreme Conscious Being. We have forgotten that we have given up our connection with that Supreme Conscious Being and that we have descended to regions of the cosmos dominated by the subtle and gross material energies: mind and gross matter. Thus, being forgetful of our original position, we attempt to dominate and enjoy those energies. For this purpose, we receive bodies made of these material energies, which are the source of all our suffering. However, being bewildered, we mistake our suffering as happiness. Driven by excessive desire and greed, we cause ecological calamities that deprive many even of their basic needs.

The Chinese people are special because they become proficient in whatever they persue. We would like to suggest that you, dear reader, steadily introduce various elements of the Bhakti Yoga practices into your own Yoga practice, especially those of *sravanam* and *kirtanam* (hearing devotional discourses and chanting Mantras). This will enrich your lessons so that you and those around you will feel increasingly inspired. In this way the Bhakti Yoga culture will naturally grow and bring happiness to the lives of countless Chinese people.

I look forward to meeting you in a place of pilgrimage.

Om tat sat!

Appendix

APPENDIX - I: CHARACTERISTICS OF THE MODES

	Ignorance	Passion	Goodness
General/ Basics	* Foolishness & madness * Illusion & sleep	* Uncontrollable desires * Intense endeavor and activities	* Sense of Duty * Happiness * Purity
Foods	Unclean & decomposed * Meat; fish; eggs; liquor	* Too bitter, sour, salty or hot; causing pain & disease	* Nourishing & healthy * Grains; fruit; vegetables
Knowledge	* Unrelated to the absolute Truth; concerned with eating & sleeping	* Considers the body to be the self; speculative doctrines & theories	* Vision of eternal soul * Sees things in relation to the whole
Understanding	* Considers illusion to be Realityand reality to be illusion	* Does not know what should be done and what should not be done	* Intelligently discriminates between what is to be feared & and not feared; what is binding and what is liberating
Action	* Irresponsible; violent; distressing to others	* Performed with great effort to satisfy one's desire to enjoy; results in distress	* Performed in knowledge as a matter of duty, without attachment
Determination	* Cannot go beyond daydreaming	* Fixed upon securing the result of the action	* Unbreakable and never deviated; in control of mind and senses
Happiness	* Comes about from sleep, laziness & illusion	* Derived from contact of the senses with their objects	* Compared to poison in the beginning but nectar at the end
Colours	* Blue; black	* Red	* White; yellow
Location	* Pub; brothel; slaughter house	* City & Town	* Forest & Natural Environment
Animals & plants	* Monkey / Funguses	* Lion / Onion; garlic	* Cow / Mango Trees
Universe	* Destruction / Shiva	* Creation / Brahma	* Maintenance / Vishnu

APPENDIX - II

YOGA LADDER

Bhagavad gita 6.3

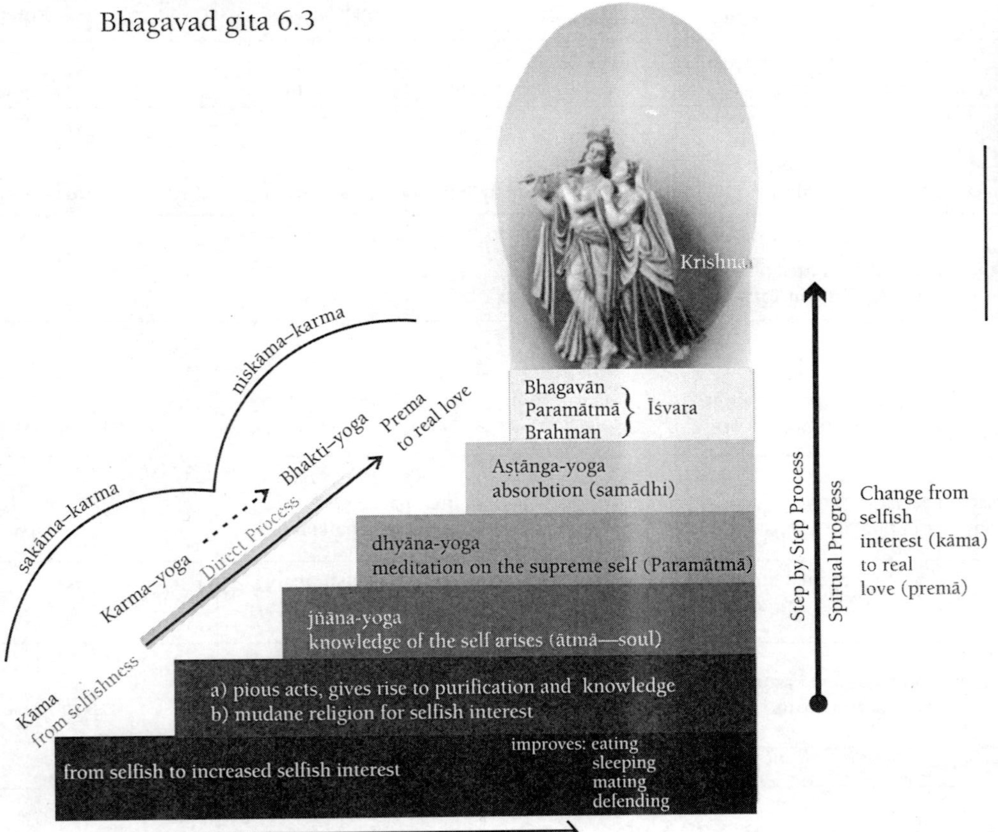

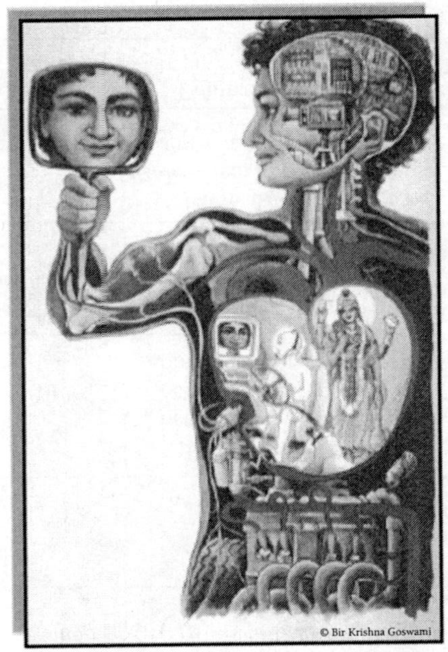

The experience "I am this body" is a delusion. By progress in Yoga one realizes "I'm the atma! As the Isvara is eternal, so am I".

APPENDIX - III:

THE "RISIKESH" CONNECTION

By grasping a faster moving tractor, a person riding on a bicycle may conveniently increase his own speed. So it goes with prayers that we learn from purified souls. Praying with the mood they developed is an essential practice in Bhakti Yoga. Here is an excerpt of a prayer taken from Bhaktivinoda Thakura (1838-1915 A. D.), a perfected Bhakti Yoga teacher who spent the last four years of his life in complete Samadhi.

The prayer is in simple Bengali. It addresses the Isvara as Gopinath and Risikesh. *Gopinath* means "Master of the Gopis," because those who are deeply absorbed in love for the Isvara, like the damsels of Vrindavan (Gopis), know Him as the dearly loved One. The Isvara is also known as Risikesh (in the Bhagavad-gita this name, which means "Master of the Senses," appears seven times), and this book, "Bhakti Yoga Pilgrimage", introduced you to the place named Risikesh. Let us build a good connection to Risikesh, to that Master who guides us in our perceptions, by entering the mood of the prayer.

Gopīnāth, anātha dekhiyā more, tumi hṛṣīkeśa, hṛṣīka damiyā, tāro 'he saṁsṛti-ghore

O Gopīnātha, You are Hṛṣīkeśa, the Lord of the senses. Seeing me so helpless, please control these senses of mine and deliver me from this dark and perilous worldly existence.

gopīnāth, sakali tomāra māyā nāhi mama bala, jñāna sunirmala, swādīna nahe e kāyā

O Gopīnātha, everything here is Your illusory energy. I have no strength or transcendental knowledge, and this body of mine is not independent, being controlled by material nature.

gopīnāth, kemone hoibe gati, prabala indriya, bośī-bhūta mana, nā chāre viṣaya-rati

O Gopīnātha, how shall I make any advancement when my mind has come under the control of the powerful senses and does not abandon its attachment to materialism?

gopīnāth, hṛdoye bosiyā mora, manake śamiyā, laho nija pāne, ghucibe vipada ghora

O Gopīnātha, after sitting down in the core of my heart and subduing my mind, please take me to You. In this way the horrible dangers of this world will disappear.

In this book, I mentioned in several places the need for mercy in order to progress. I referred to the chanting of the Maha-mantra: Hare Krishna, Hare Krishna, Krishna Krishna, Hare Hare; Hare Rama, Hare Rama; Rama Rama, Hare Hare. Chant this simple mantra and try to imbibe the mood of the above prayer, regularly reviewing these Yoga teachings - and see what happens.

WHAT IS WRONG WITH IMPERSONALISM?

Renowned sages, mystics and philosophers in many cultures and eras have experienced and recorded comparable perceptions about the nature of Ultimate Reality. They disclose that the phenomenal world is not the only reality; another non-physical reality exists. The perception of such Yogis and mystics throughout the ages are considered to be valid because of their consistency and similarities, despite their cultural differences. Patanjali, Buddha or then Lao-tzu, Plotinus, Meister Eckhart or in more recent times Aldous Huxley, all stand as a testimony for the existence of such a "perennial Truth."

In recent years, modern physics is confronted with the same mystery and moves towards the identical conclusion; namely, that a singular entity is the original source of the order which unifies and underlies all manifested forms and qualities. Fritjof Capra in his *Tao of Physics* postulates this idea by referring to Quantum Physics as does Physicist Mani Bhaumik in his best seller *Code Name God - the Spiritual Odyssey of a Man of Science.*

Oddly, Bhaumik objects to the notion of "Nothing is Real" and "Nothingness" and states with confidence that what we see and experience *does exist*, but only as organized energies: "Your dog, or your car, or your spouse.... Durga, Kali, Krishna, Shiva, and all the myriad personages of the Indian repertory company, they are but embodiments of Brahman." When Brahman is covered by *maya*, the illusion of individual existence arises. However, ultimately, we will again be dissolved into it.

For Bhaumik, we exist temporarily and will "become one with the One." The dilemma is; if individuality is an illusion, what is the meaning of "does exist"? With this type of understanding, "we exist" seems to be true only as long we are in illusion. The "I" is not seen as real. Neither so is the Isvara, Krishna.[1]

1 Mani Bhaumik's ideas are not new. A certain branch of Yoga teachers, although speaking about the Isvara, have no personal conception of Him and consider the impersonal Brahman to be the underlying cause of all there is: "The word "Isvara" popularly known as "God" has a peculiar meaning in the Advaita philosophy. The Vedantist does not believe Isvara to be the absolute existence, because He is as unreal as the phenomenal universe. Brahman associated with ignorance is known as Isvara. The difference between Isvara and the ordinary man is that the former, though associated with Maya, is not bound by its fetters, whereas the latter is its slave. Isvara is the highest manifestation of Brahman in the phenomenal-universe". Quoted from: Sadananda, The Vedantasara. Edited with notes and indeces by Colonel G.A. Jacob. Fifth edition, revised. Bombay 1934. Soft covers. Page 28

According to Bhaumik, spiritual less experienced persons ascribe personhood and individuality to the Absolute Truth. When one is advanced, one will dump this view and achieve a timeless, mystical experience. "Could it be", he then questions, concluding his book, "that the timeless mystical experience of oneness with the source, an experience that transcends all faiths and cultures, is actually the closest we humans can ever come to perceiving the universe as it truly is?"

Here the Bhakti Yoga teachers voice an empathic "No" - oneness is not the closest we can get: It is half way only. Wrongly postulating oneness to be the Ultimate Reality deprives people from understanding Bhakti Yoga. It is a disservice to mankind.

I apologies for the insistent objection to the impersonal view, and you might deem it to be excessive. However, I know of a multitude of Yoga teachers, throughout the ages who, by their spiritual realization, describe the source of this phenomenal world as having variety, form, activities and eternal individuality. In other words they say that our world here is a reflection of the eternal world and what exists here exists only because it exists there, although there it is without the limitations of matter. I strongly feel this should be known to everyone. By knowing one has a chance for victory over repeated birth and death and one will consequently not hold on to a half way understanding that leads nowhere.

Our reasoning can show that the Supreme has transcendental individuality, but it cannot tell us the specific, concrete facts about that Individual. Whatever is in the effect is in the cause and so we can conclude that "I-ness" must necessarily be with the Supreme since we find it in the world of *maya*. At this point we have to drop our efforts to understand the Isvara by our own mental prowess, and we have to hear, submissively, from the advanced Bhakti-Yogis. They disclose in full the specific name, form, opulence, and activities of the Supreme, which are beyond the effulgence of impersonal Brahman: it is Krishna, the all-attractive, whose transcendental bluish-black form glows like a new raincloud illuminated by lightning, whose jewel-bedecked hands lift a silver flute to His lips, whose eyes, beautiful like lotus petals, roam restless with love over His devotees in the eternal spiritual kingdom.

When the Impersonalists hear about that form beyond the effulgence, the transcendental form of Krishna, the embodiment of all beauty, they think of it as material, as *maya*. This is likely because their mentality is so rigidly materialistic. They are unable to accept the notion of "transcendental form" because as far as they are concerned all form is material. They appeal to the idea that the Supreme must be unlimited and unconditioned. And all form, according to them, is a limitation - likewise, individuality is considered a limitation. But why should we impose our material ideas (paradigms) of form and personality on the transcendental realm? Who says that all form has to be material form? Who says that there is no spiritual form and personality?

We can agree that the Supreme must be unlimited great. It is paradoxical that the impersonal conception of the Supreme, arrived at by relentless denial, is of an entity so systematically stripped of everything - form, attributes, and relations - that it is essentially no different from the idea of nothing at all. On the other hand, the personal conception of Isvara as a being full of transcendental or limitless spiritual forms, qualities, activities, and individuality really does indicate one who is the greatest of all.[2]

Let me remind you of a confidential fact about the Isvara: although He is neutral and equally disposed to all beings, He is nonetheless partial to those who approach Him in love (Bhakti). He is sentient and responds to Bhakti. Thus, an unfortunate person turns into a most fortunate one, because by the Isvara's benevolence, such a person is progressively freed from karmic reactions. Looking at the world today with its huge accumulated and collective Karma that turns into a variety of suffering we can understand that we require the mercy of the Isvara, perhaps more than ever.

2 The reasoning is adapted from: BtG # 15- 07, 1980 *Yoga Mush and the Jerk Divine* by Ravindra Svarupa Das

Glossary

GLOSSARY

A

Advaita —Oneness (from *a*, "not", and *dvaita*, "duality"). The system of Vedānta philosophy put forward by Śaṅkarācārya is known as Advaita Vedānta. It argues for a monistic, impersonal absolute truth.

Ajāmila—a fallen brāhmaṇa who was saved from hell by unintentionally chanting the Isvara's name at the time of death.

Arjuna— An eternal associate of Kṛishna. Kṛishna became his chariot driver and spoke the Bhagavad-gītā to him on the battlefield of Kurukṣetra.

Asat—not eternal, temporary.

Aṣṭāṅga-yoga—the eightfold system of mystic yoga, propounded by Patañjali, meant for realizing the presence of the Paramātmā in the heart.

Ātmā—the self (refers to the soul)

B

Bhakti-yoga—the system of cultivation of bhakti, or pure devotional
Service

Bhagavad-gītā—a seven-hundred verse record of a conversation between Lord Kṛṣṇa and His disciple, Arjuna, from the Bhīṣma Parva of the Mahābhārata of Vedavyāsa. The conversation took place in the midst of two armies minutes before the start of an immense fratricidal battle. In this conversation, Kṛṣṇa teaches the science of the Absolute Truth and the importance of devotional service to the despondent Arjuna; and it contains the essence of all Vedic wisdom. Śrīla Prabhupāda's annotated English translation is called Bhagavad-gītā As It Is.

Brahm—the first created living being and secondary creator of the
material universe. His life span is more than 311 trillion of our years

Brahmaloka—the highest planet of the universe, that of the demigod Brahmā

Brahman—(1) the infinitesimal spiritual individual soul; (2) the impersonal, allpervasive aspect of the Supreme.

Buddhi-yoga—(buddhi-intelligence + yoga-mystic elevation) another term for bhaktiyoga

C

Caitanya Mahāprabhu, (1486-1534)—He appeared in Navadvīpa, West Bengal, and inaugurated the congregational chanting of the holy names of the Lord to teach pure Bhakti Yoga by means of Saṅkīrtana.

D

Demigods—universal controllers and residents of the higher planets. The Sanskrit equivalent is deva or devata. Demigods are jīvas whom the īśvara empowers to represent Him in the management of the universe. The first of the demigods is Brahmā. Indra is the demigod of rain, Sūrya of the sunshine, Candra of the moonshine, Varuṇa of water. There are thirty-three million demigods in all. They live in the upper regions of the universe called svarga, or heaven. Less intelligent people worship the demigods through karma-kāṇḍa rituals to get material blessings in this life, and to be granted entrance into svarga in the next life. In the Bhagavad-gītā, Lord Kṛṣṇa condemns demigod worship as being avidhi-pūrvaka, against the true purpose of the Vedas.

Dharma—one's natural occupation. The Sanskrit term dharma is variously translated as duty, virtue, morality, righteousness, or religion, but no single English word conveys the whole meaning of dharma.

Dhruva Mahārāja—a great devotee who at the age of five performed severe austerities and realized the Supreme.

G

Guru—spiritual master; literally, this term means "heavy." The spiritual master is called guru because he is heavy with knowledge.

H

Hṛṣīkeśa—a name of Kṛṣṇa meaning "the master of all senses." Also a place of pilgrimage situated on the foot of the Himalaya.

I

Īśopaniṣad—one of the 108 principal Vedic scriptures known as the Upaniṣads.

Īśvara—a controller. Kṛṣṇa is parameśvara, the supreme controller; the atma has the power to choose whether to surrender to the īśvara or not. If he does surrender, he is freed from bondage of karma. If he does not, he is bound to the cycle of birth and death (saṁsāra).

J

Jīva (jīvātmā)—the living entity, who is an eternal soul, individual but part and parcel of the Supreme.

Jñāna—knowledge. Material jñāna does not go beyond the material body. Transcendental jñāna discriminates between matter and spirit. Perfect jñāna is knowledge of the body, the soul, and the Supreme.

Jñānī—one who is engaged in the cultivation of knowledge (especially by philosophical speculation). In Vedic terminology, there is jñāna and vijñāna. Jñāna refers to the knowledge of the self as not the body, whereas vijñāna refers to knowledge of the self's relationship to the Supreme Self.

Jñāna-kāṇḍa—The path of philosophical speculation.

K

Kaivalya—the impersonal liberation of merging into the spiritual effulgence; final isolation of the atma from matter.

Kali-yuga—the "Age of Quarrel and Hypocrisy; " the fourth and last age in the cycle of four yugas. This is the present age in which we are now living. It began 5,000 years ago and lasts for a total of 432,000 years. It is characterized by materialism and stringent material miseries.

Karma-kāṇḍa—the division of the Vedas which deals with fruitive activities performed for the purpose of gradual purification of the grossly entangled materialist

Karma-yoga—action in devotional service; the path of self realization through dedicating the fruits of one's work to the Isvara.

Kīrtana—Narrating or singing the glories of the Supreme; the devotional process of chanting the names and glories of the Isvara. A related Sanskrit word is kīrti (fame). Hence, kīrtana means to glorify, and saṅkīrtana means to glorify congregationally the fame of the Supreme. Saṅkīrtana is the yuga-dharma, or the main spiritual occupation and means of deliverance for the present age of Kali.

L

Līlā—a transcendental "pastime" or activity performed by the Isvara; The endlessly expanding spiritual activities and pastimes of Kṛṣṇa

M

Māyā—illusion; that which is not, unreality, deception, forgetfulness, material illusion. Under illusion a man thinks he can be happy in this temporary phenomena world. The nature of the phenomenal world is that the more a man tries to exploit the material situation, the more he is bound by māyā's complexities; The material bewilderment of the living entity begins with his attraction to the glare of the brahmajyoti. That attraction leads to his entanglement in the modes of material nature.

Muni—a sage or self-realized soul.

Mahā-mantra—the great chant for deliverance: Hare Kṛṣṇa, Hare Kṛṣṇa, Kṛṣṇa Kṛṣṇa, Hare Hare Hare Rāma, Hare Rāma, Rāma Rāma, Hare Hare; composed of the principal names of the Isvara in their vocative forms. This maha-mantra is found in the Purāṇas and Upaniṣads and is specifically recommended for chanting in this age of Kali as the means of spiritual progress.

N

Niṣkāma—free from material desires.

P

Paramātmā—the Supersoul, the localized aspect of the Isvara residing in the heart of each embodied living entity and pervading all of material nature.

Pradhāna—the total material energy in its unmanifest state; The unmanifest (avyakta) material nature

Purāṇas—the eighteen major and eighteen minor Vedic literatures compiled about five thousand years ago in India by Vedavyasa relating the histories of this and other planets.

Puruṣa—the enjoyer, or male; person or soul. This term may be applied to both the atma and the Supreme.

S

Sādhu—holy person.

Sakāma—with material desires.

Samādhi—total absorption and trance of the mind and senses in consciousness of the Supreme. The word samādhi also refers to the tomb where a great soul's body is laid after his departure from this world.

Saṁhitās—supplementary Vedic literatures expressing the conclusions of particular self-realized authorities.

Sanskrit—the oldest language in the world. Sanskrit is an ancient language of culture, learning and spiritual wisdom. The Vedas are all written in Sanskrit.

Śiva—superintendent of the mode of ignorance (tama-guṇa); takes charge of destroying the universe at the time of annihilation. He is confused by some with the Supreme Isvara.

Siddhis—mystic perfections usually acquired by yoga practice and natural to the residents of Siddhaloka

Sravaṇam—hearing from an authorized source.

Śruti—knowledge via hearing; the original Vedic scriptures, the Vedas and Upaniṣads.

Svargaloka—the heavenly planets or abodes of the demigods in the phenomenal world.

U

Upaniṣads—one-hundred and eight Sanskrit treatises that embody the philosophy of the Vedas. Considered the most significant philosophical sections and crest jewels of the Vedas.

V

Vaikuṇṭha—the eternal planets of the spiritual world which lies beyond the coverings of the material universe. Literally, "the place with no anxiety."

Viṣṇu—Viṣṇu supervises the maintenance of the created universe, and enters into the material universe before creation. Literally, the all-pervading, the Supersoul.

Vṛndāvana—the topmost transcendental abode of Krishna, the Supreme Lord, where He fully manifests His quality of sweetness; the village on this earth where He enacted His childhood pastimes five housand years ago; His personal spiritual abode descended to the earthly plane, situated on the western bank of the river Yamunā.

ACKNOWLEDGEMENTS / CREDITS

The outline of Astanga-Yoga in Chapter Four has been shaped by the works of Suhotra Maharaja.

The Yoga Ladder concept in Chapter Five and the insight into the principles of "free-will" in Chapter Eight are adapted from Bhurijan Das's works. His published books include *The Art of Teaching*, *Surrender Unto Me* (an in-depth study of the Bhagavad-gita), *My Glorious Master* and *Unveiling His Lotus Feet* (an in-depth study of the *Srimad-Bhagavatam*).

The concept of paradigms in Chapter Ten and the proper use of language in Chapter Sixteen are adapted from transcripts of lectures given by William H. Deadwyler (Ravindra Svarupa Das) who holds an M.A. and Ph.D. in Religion from Temple University and a B.A. in philosophy from the University of Pennsylvania.

In Chapter Fourteen two paragraphs about creation are adapted from Michael A. Cremo (Drutakarma Das). Michael Cremo is a member of the History of Science Society, the World Archeological Congress, the Philosophy of Science Association, the European Association of Archaeologists, and an associate member of the Bhaktivedanta Institute specializing in the history and philosophy of science.

Much of the research on Yoga and Buddhism for Chapter Six was done by Steven Rosen (Satyaraja Das), an author of some twenty books on *Veda*-related subjects. He is the editor-in-chief of the *Journal of Vaishnava Studies*, a peer-refereed academic journal, which focuses on the culture and philosophy of Vaishnava-Hinduism.

My humble gratitude goes to all these experts and to the Bhaktivedanta Book Trust (BBT) for the use of verses and purports from the copyrighted books of Srila Prabhupada. All such verses and purports are the intellectual property of Bhaktivedanta Book Trust, ©BBT.

This book, *Bhakti Yoga Pilgrimage - What Patanjali and Buddha Did Not Teach*, is the fruit of love and care of countless mentors on my spiritual journey, first and foremost my initiating teacher, His Holiness Lokanath Swami Maharaj.

ARTS AND PHOTOGRAPHY

Photos: Bhurijan Das; Lohitaksa Das; Sankirtan Das

Line Drawings: Svetlana Makarova

Cover design: Sparsh Communications

BIBLIOGRAPHY (WORKS CITED)

BBT Books ©BBT: Bhagavad-gita; Srimad Bhagavatam; Caitanya Caritamrita; Beyond Birth and Death; Isopanishad; Brahma-samhita; Nectar of Devotion; Message of Godhead; Endless Love

Others: Bhurijan Das: Surrender unto Me; My Glorious Master; VTE Study Guide

Quoted: Yoga Sutra; Vedanta Sutra; Katha Upanishad; Brihad-aranyaka Upanisad; Mundaka Upanishad; Chandogya Upanishad

AUTHOR

Sankirtan Das, 48, was born in Switzerland and has been practicing Bhakti Yoga since 1986 in Australia. Sankirtan Das has gathered much of his experience about Yoga in India, where he has been living with Yoga masters since 1990. He holds a degree as Bhakti Yoga teacher from the VIHE (Vrindavan Institute for Higher Education), where he regularly teaches. After learning basic Chinese he functions for a travel agent from Beijing by taking Chinese tour groups to holy places in India and the Himalayan Mountains. Contact: Sankirtana.lok@pamho.net and www.walk4cows.net

Index

INDEX

Boat across Yamuna

Ghat at Haridwar